Helicopter Pilot's Handbook of Mountain Flying and Advanced Techniques

Helicopter Pilot's Handbook of Mountain Flying and Advanced Techniques

Norman Bailey

Airlife
England

First published in 2002 by
Airlife Publishing, an imprint of
The Crowood Press Ltd
Ramsbury, Marlborough
Wiltshire SN8 2HR

www.crowood.com

This impression 2004

© Norman Bailey 2002

All rights reserved. No part of this publication may be reproduced or transmitted in any form or by any means, electronic or mechanical, including photocopy, recording, or any information storage and retrieval system, without permission in writing from the publishers.

British Library Cataloguing-in-Publication Data
A catalogue record for this book is available from the British Library.

ISBN 1 84307 321 0

Typeset by Phoenix Typesetting, Auldgirth, Dumfriesshire

Printed and bound in Great Britain by The Cromwell Press Ltd, Trowbridge, Wiltshire

CONTENTS

Part One, Mountain Flying

Introduction **2**

Medical Factors Disappearance of Normal Horizon **3**   Vertigo **3**   Apprehension **4**   Oxygen **4**

Helicopter Considerations Engine **5**   Airframe **5**   Rotors **5**   Tail Rotor **5**   Retreating Blade Stall **6**   Flight Controls **6**   Airspeed Indicator **6**

Mountain Winds Wind Behaviour **7**   Light **8**   Medium **8**   Strong **8**   Venturi Effect **10**   Regular Slopes **10**   Uneven Slopes **11**   Multiple Ridges **12**   Sharp Contours **12**   Area of Nil or Zero Wind **13**   Turbulence and Downdraughts **13**   Standing Waves **13**   Rotor Streaming Turbulence **14**

Flight Preparation Study of Maps **16**   Study of Meteorological Conditions **16**   Study of Helicopter Performance Charts **16**

En Route in the Mountains Wind Assessment **17**   Turbulence Penetration Airspeed **17**   Blade Stall **17**   Engine Failure **17**   Downdraughts **17**

Landing Sites Power Margin **19**   Wind Direction and Behaviour **19**   Constant Airspeed/Constant Power **20**   Cloverleaf Pattern **20**   The Reconnaissance **21**   The High Reconnaissance **21**   The Low Reconnaissance **22**   The Circuit **22**

Approaches and Take-offs 23   Approach Speed **24**   The Landing **24**   The Take-off **25**

Flying along Slopes 26   Landing Sites on Slopes **27**   Reconnaissance of Slope Sites **27**   Approaches to the Slope **28**

Crests and Pinnacles Crossing a Crest Line **29**   Flight over Crests from the Windward Side **29**   Flight over Crests from the Lee Side **30**   Approaches to Crests and Peaks **30**   No Wind **30**   Strong Wind **30**   Take-offs **32**

Flight in and along Valleys 33   Landing Sites **34**   Reconnaissance **34**   Approaches and Take-offs **34**

Flights through a Col 36

Effects of Sun and Shadow 37

Common Faults 38

Part Two, Advanced Flying Techniques

Helicopter Weight and Balance 40   Weight and Balance Calculation **46**

Underslung Loads 49

Night Operations 56

Forced Landings and Ditching 63

Winter Operations 70

Visual Searches 73

Winching 75

THE HELICOPTER PILOT'S HANDBOOK

Part One

Mountain Flying

Introduction

At some time or another, many helicopter pilots will wish to experience the thrill and enjoyment of mountain flying. Safe operation in mountainous terrain and unpredictable weather requires an awareness of and feel for conditions that can only be gained from experience. Hopefully, these notes will go a long way towards helping pilots establish a strong foundation for safe operations on which they can build as experience is gained.

Medical Factors

When first operating a helicopter in mountainous areas, the majority of pilots are affected by some or all of the psychological effects outlined below. These effects diminish as confidence increases, but a knowledge of what to expect is the best guarantee of flight safety.

DISAPPEARANCE OF NORMAL HORIZON

In mountainous country a helicopter will often fly below the level of the surrounding terrain, depriving the pilot of his normal horizon. Frequent cross-reference to flight instruments is essential in these conditions, to prevent exaggerated helicopter attitudes as a result of trying to level the aircraft by reference to nearby ridge lines.

Loss of attitude appreciation can also make the assessment of ground slopes inaccurate. If possible, when judging a slope, flight instruments should be used to check that the helicopter is laterally level when near the slope.

VERTIGO

Vertigo can be experienced when sudden and dramatic changes in height occur. Hovering at 5,000 feet with a definite horizon may produce no ill effects, but an approach on to a pinnacle with a sheer drop on all sides can easily lead to disorientation and tenseness on the controls.

APPREHENSION

Apprehension, even fear, leading to indecision and tenseness on the controls is quite normal until the confidence bred by experience and knowledge of a wide variety of situations is gained.

OXYGEN

Modern helicopters are capable of sustained operations above 10,000 feet yet do not carry oxygen. Insufficient oxygen under these conditions will lead to confusion, shortage of breath, poor judgement and a false feeling of confidence.

Helicopter Considerations

Regardless of the height of the mountains, it is the **density altitude (DA)** which affects flying the most. In simple terms, it is found by setting 1,013 millibars on the altimeter and reading off the **pressure altitude (PA)**, which is then used in the following formula:
$DA = PA \pm (120T)$, where T is the difference between actual and ICAN temperature.
Example: Operating at FL 75, OAT + 10°C
        (ICAN temperature at 7,500 feet = zero)
        $DA = 7,500 + (120 \times 10)$
            $= 8,700$ feet
   Density altitude affects the helicopter as follows:

ENGINE

With both the piston and turbine engine, power is reduced with increased DA, thus giving less reserve power. All manoeuvres such as quick stops, steep turns, etc, should therefore be avoided.

AIRFRAME

The induced power required will increase as air density falls. The effect is greatest at low speed, and falls as indicated airspeed (IAS) rises. As a result the power margin will decrease with altitude.

ROTORS

Regardless of altitude, the rotor turns at the same TAS. It follows, therefore, that as altitude increases a higher pitch setting is required. This means that there is less collective available to cushion any landing. Always maintain maximum rotor RPM and handle the controls smoothly and carefully.

TAIL ROTOR

Pedal displacement will be increased for two reasons; to balance the increased torque from the main rotor and to produce the necessary thrust in the less dense air. This means that less pedal control is available. Again, maintain maximum main rotor RPM and avoid any rapid yawing movements.

RETREATING BLADE STALL

The increased pitch angles used as altitude increases bring the retreating blade closer to its stalling angle. A sharp vertical gust could cause a sudden and severe blade stall, making the helicopter pitch sharply nose-up and roll towards the retreating side of the disc. The risk of blade stall from turbulence and manoeuvring can be minimised by flying at minimum power speed where necessary. The maximum permissible true airspeed (TAS), as well as IAS, is reduced with altitude.

FLIGHT CONTROLS

The response of all the flying controls reduces with altitude owing to the decreasing air density and gives a feeling of lag or sloppiness. Larger movements of the cyclic stick are required to effect attitude changes and the collective lever position will be higher because a higher pitch angle is required to produce the required rotor thrust. The tail rotor blades have to work at an increased pitch angle thus limiting the pedal control available to the pilot.

AIRSPEED INDICATOR

As altitude increases, the dynamic pressure applied to the airspeed indicator (ASI) is reduced for any given TAS. The IAS will therefore read less than the TAS as altitude is gained. All pilots must familiarise themselves with the flight envelope pattern shown in the Flight Manual, and fly within it.

Mountain Winds

Without doubt, the major factor affecting mountain operations is the lack of available actual weather information to enable accurate predictions of wind speed and strength to be made. Wind behaviour in a small geographical area can vary considerably, making direction, vertical motion and turbulence unpredictable.

Air flowing against an obstruction will rise up the windward side and be compressed by the following air. Any turbulence will tend to diminish, but the air will accelerate. As it flows over the top of the obstruction, the air again accelerates owing to venturi action. At some point, depending on the curvature of the feature, the laminar flow breaks down and becomes turbulent. This point is called the **transition point**. Usually a clearly defined plane is formed on the one side of which the air is smooth and updraughting and on the other side it is turbulent and eventually downdraughting. This plane is called the **demarcation line**.

The angle of the demarcation line becomes steeper as the wind increases.

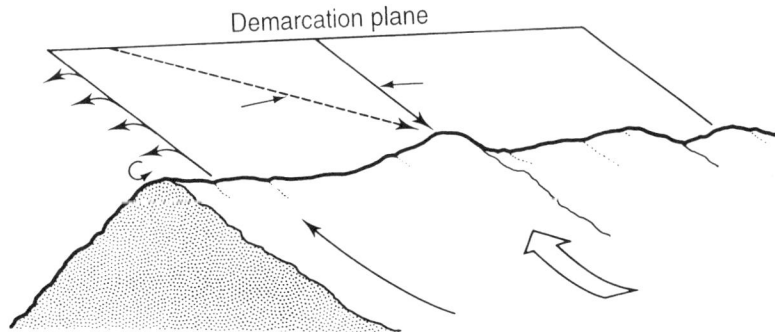

WIND BEHAVIOUR

No hard and fast rules can be laid down, as the actual wind behaviour depends on many variable factors such as slope, surface irregularity, shape of peaks, air stability, etc. However, the general behaviour can be considered for three major windspeed bands:

THE HELICOPTER PILOT'S HANDBOOK

Light (0–15 kts)

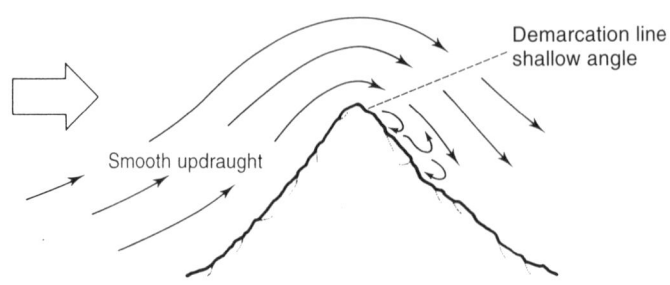

Medium (15–30 kts)

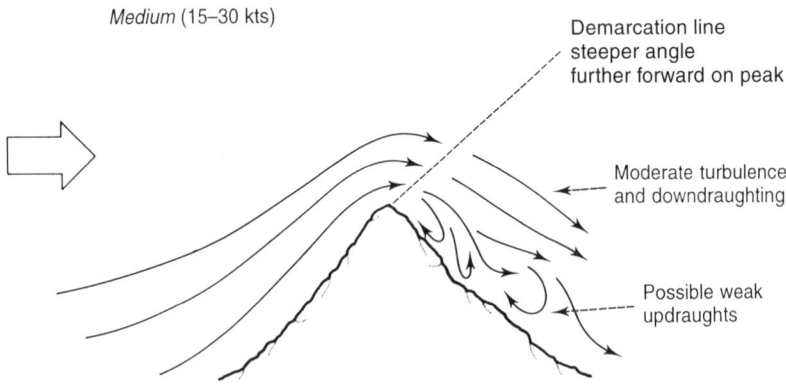

Strong (30 kts plus)

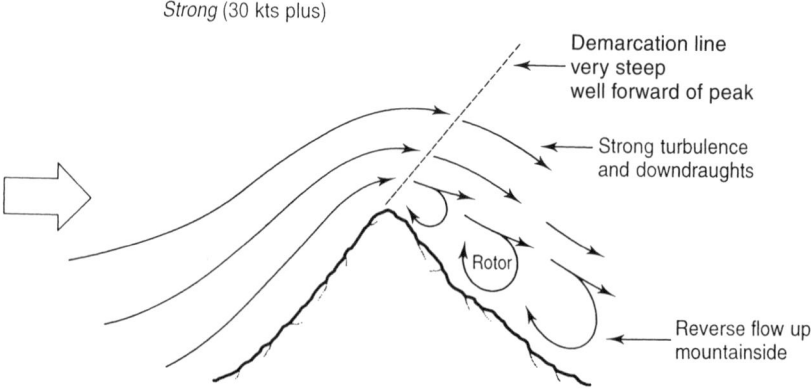

Close to the ground the air moves in a **laminar flow**, but the depth of the laminar section and the **gust spread** varies considerably depending on the nature of the surface and surface heating.

On passing over or round an obstacle, the air may become turbulent or formed into **rolls** which may have a horizontal or vertical axis.

Turbulence caused by the shape of the ground:

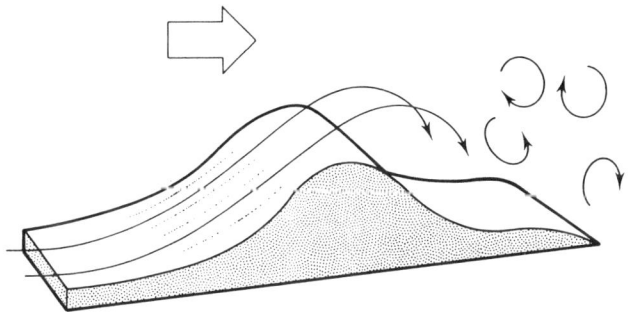

Roll with a vertical axis, often found near pinnacles or isolated hills:

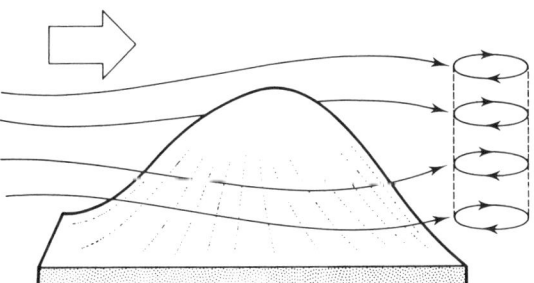

Roll with a horizontal axis, often found near crest lines:

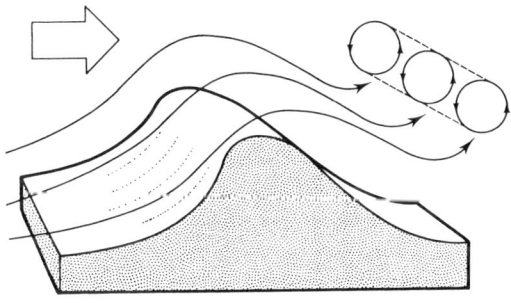

VENTURI EFFECT

The movement of air over a crest line creates a **venturi effect** and results in an increased wind speed over the summit.

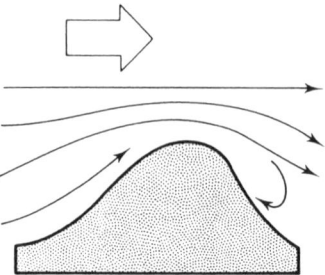

This phenomenon is accompanied by a reduction of pressure which can cause the altimeter to over-read slightly. The venturi effect is even more marked when found in a valley or col, where the venturi is more clearly defined.

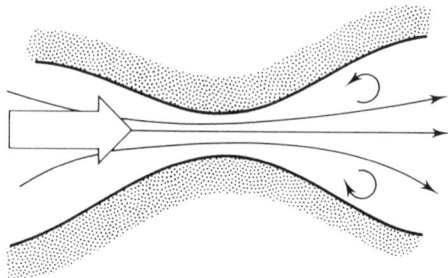

REGULAR SLOPES

A light wind blowing up a feature with a regular surface and a moderate slope, (up to 40°) will accelerate slightly on the up slope, giving rise to a gentle updraught. It will follow the line of the contour over the crest and, at some point past the crest, turn into a gentle downdraught. At some point below the summit on the lee side, a roll is likely to form. Air rises beyond the crest, and rolls form near the bottom.

The effects become more marked as the wind strength increases. The updraughts will increase, as will the downdraughts and turbulence. The demarcation line between the up- and downdraught will move upwind and closer to the crest. The venturi effect over the crest will probably start to show.

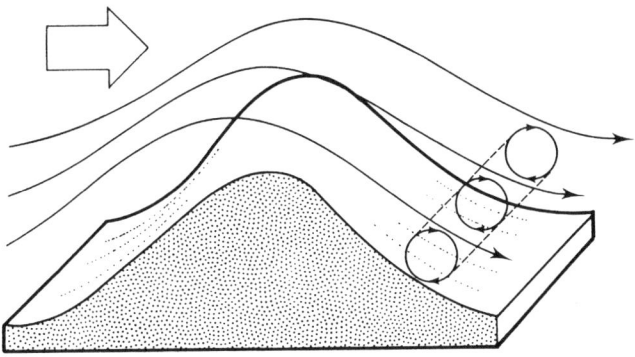

UNEVEN SLOPES

The effect of wind blowing over an uneven slope is to create turbulence on the up slope as well as on the down slope. The stronger the wind, the greater the effect.

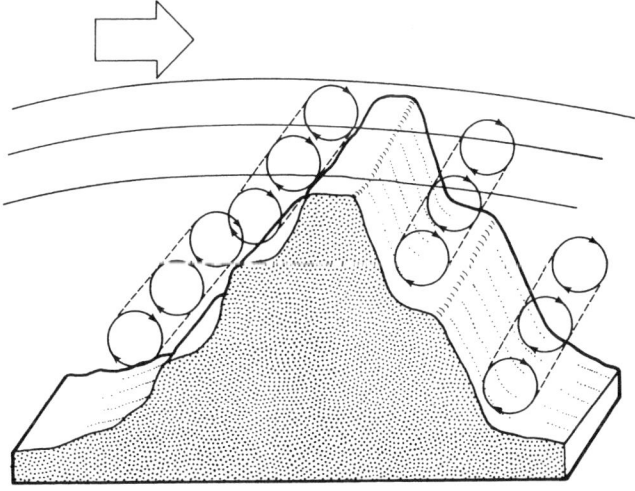

Strong turbulence created by uneven ground may be found on either side of the ridge.

MULTIPLE RIDGES

When wind blows across a series of ridges, the effect is to form rolls between the crest lines. This may cause a dangerous situation to arise in which downdraughts may exist on an up slope where you would normally expect an updraught.

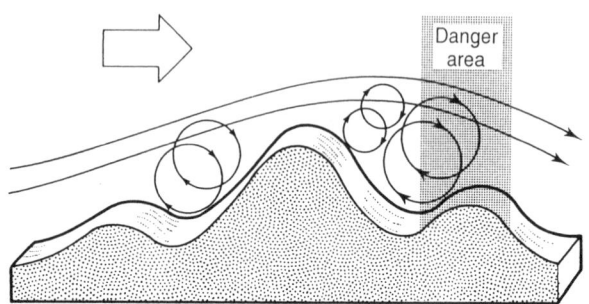

SHARP CONTOURS

For the same wind speeds, the up- and downdraughts and turbulence across sharp contours will be more severe than with ground of a more gentle shape. The demarcation line will move to the windward edge and eddying, reverse winds or an area of no wind can be expected behind the demarcation line. Thus, the safest landing area will probably be found on the windward edge, where, because of unsuitable landing surface, it may be necessary to land back from the edge. The pilot must now be prepared for a landing in an area of no wind or of reverse wind.

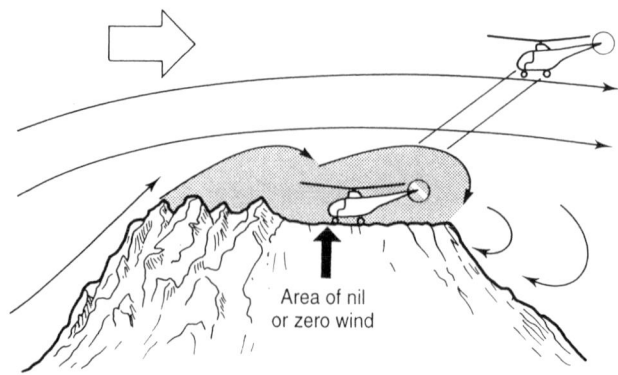

AREA OF NIL OR ZERO WIND

This area of no wind is not high and it is difficult to locate during the pre-landing reconnaissance. However, should a landing have to be made back from the demarcation line, the loss of wind effect, or even the presence of a reverse wind, must be anticipated. Because of this danger, a pilot should only approach to a point where a landing can be made.

Once the helicopter has arrived in the hover, avoid hovering over areas which are not suitable for landing because of the danger of being forced on to the ground. In any case, you should never hover away from the demarcation line, although you may need to move forward towards it to obtain a better position for the take-off.

TURBULENCE AND DOWNDRAUGHTS

Areas of turbulence and downdraughts will be found on almost every flight made into the mountains. Their influence is dangerous and should not be underestimated. As well as the fatigue imposed on the airframe, violent turbulence can give momentary loss of control, such as blade stall caused by entering a violent updraught.

The precautions to be taken in these conditions are:

Always maintain maximum permissible RRPM;

Fly at climbing speed. This will give maximum reserve of power, less dissymmetry of lift with less likelihood of blade stall and use of a low pitch angle with less likelihood of blade stall.

The strength of a downdraught will often easily exceed the climbing speed of a helicopter. A rapid reduction of airspeed is usually the first indication of entering a downdraught. **This must be corrected immediately.**

Downdraughts are likely to be found when approaching peaks and crests and the angle of approach should be steepened accordingly.

STANDING WAVES

A standing wave should occur when the following conditions are met:

Unstable air in the lower layer above the ground.

Strong surface and gradient winds increasing with height.

A mountain range barrier to provide upward deviation of the air flow.

A stable layer at a height roughly two to three times the height of the barrier above the mountains.

This gives rise to the following effects in the lee of the mountain range:
Wave undulation to the lee, with turbulence in the troughs of the waves.
Reverse winds below the waves.
Localised but strong increases in windspeed.

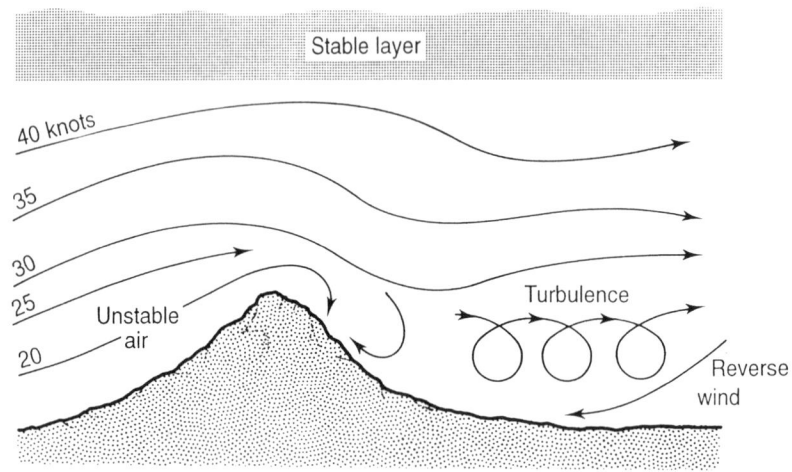

As can be seen from the above diagram, these conditions can produce some marked up- and downdraughting conditions with turbulence well clear of the mountains themselves.

ROTOR STREAMING TURBULENCE

Rotor streaming is a comparatively rare occurrence but one which produces very severe turbulence to the lee of a mountain range. The conditions necessary for it to form are:
Unstable air in the lower levels above the ground.
A stable layer at two to three times the height of the mountain range.
A strong surface and gradient wind decreasing markedly with height in and above the stable layer.
A mountain range to provide the upward deflection of the airflow.
When these conditions are present, the strong airflow starts to wave upwards on the lee side, meets the slack winds and shears back on itself, forming a rotary circulation. The stable layer acts as a lid, holding down the upward flow of air, and assists the circulation. This rotary circulation causes a marked increase in wind strength downwind, with severe turbulence.

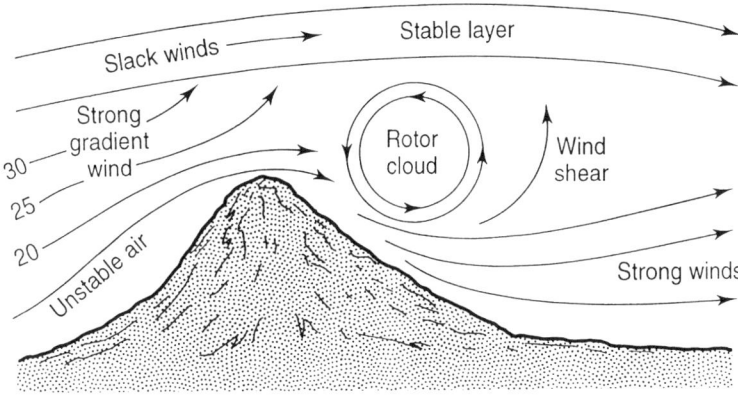

The circulation can cover a wide area to the lee of the mountain range and will lie in a roll along the lee side. If sufficient moisture is present a roll of cloud known as a **rotor cloud** can be formed, running through the axis of circulation. The cloud will be found to be rolling about its axis and is typified by broken, straggling tendrils around its edges. It often has quite a marked vertical movement.

A knowledge of the behaviour of winds in the mountains will give the pilot some idea of which areas are likely to be safe for helicopter flying and which are likely to be dangerous or unfavourable. It is impossible to give examples to cover all cases owing to the complexity of the patterns caused by the shape of the ground, the strength of the wind, turbulence and downdraughts. The only rule is to be extremely careful in all manoeuvres.

Flight Preparation

The pilot who fully understands airflow in mountainous areas will plan and fly each trip to avoid regions of downdraughting air and turbulence. He will also deliberately use areas of updraughts to fly at lower power settings and thus reduce blade pitch angles. Pre-flight planning should take into consideration the following:

STUDY OF MAPS

Maps should be studied to determine the heights of intended landing areas and whether landing on them appears possible, the position of crests, valleys, obstacles and terrain generally, and diversion routes in case of weather deterioration or emergencies.

STUDY OF METEOROLOGICAL CONDITIONS

Pay particular attention to cloud base, visibility and trends. Know with certainty the general direction of the wind at the height at which the helicopter will be operating. Check the temperature at this height as well, so that the density altitude can be forecast.

STUDY OF HELICOPTER PERFORMANCE CHARTS

Study the performance charts in the Flight Manual. It is imperative that pilots know in advance the maximum weight which can be taken to a given altitude, the maximum altitude for a given weight, the hover ceiling for any given weight both in ground effect (IGE) and out of ground effect (OGE), the cruising speed to be adopted as a function of all-up weight (AUW) and altitude, and the risk of blade stall and other critical conditions which might be encountered. The choice of your transit route will depend mainly on the meteorological forecast for the period.

En Route in the Mountains

WIND ASSESSMENT

During the transit, wind and turbulence should be continually assessed and the route varied as necessary. Smoke, trees, birds, cloud shadows, drift and groundspeed, etc, all provide valuable indications to the observant pilot.

TURBULENCE PENETRATION AIRSPEED

In turbulence, any airspeed between 70 and 80 kts, (minimum power speed) is acceptable. However, if the level of turbulence increases this should be reduced accordingly.

BLADE STALL

To avoid blade stall, try not to fly at high pitch angles, especially if sharp vertical gusts are anticipated. If blade stall does occur, reduce collective pitch first and then airspeed.

ENGINE FAILURE

The wise pilot will always consider the possibility of engine failure and fly so as to minimise the risks. Where possible, fly at a safe height, within reach of a reasonable landing area, and avoid crossing close to sheer faces. In the event of an engine failure, make the best use of any available landing areas, ensuring that, whatever else happens, the helicopter does not roll down the mountainside.

DOWNDRAUGHTS

It is difficult to be particular about the best action to take if a helicopter encounters a powerful downdraught. Generally speaking, however, the pilot should apply full power, fly at climbing speed and turn with the downdraught away from the feature causing it, choosing a downhill route towards a clear area. The high ground speed should be disregarded and a close watch kept on the airspeed indicator. Try to regain altitude in the ascending air on a lifting slope.

If it appears that the helicopter will be forced into the ground, remember that the downdraught will reduce in severity somewhere near the valley floor. Make for the most favourable area, maintaining the best rate of climb speed and full power. Turn into wind and choose as flat a landing site as possible. If the ground is sloping, try and head up the slope. On most occasions a touchdown can be avoided by using an escape route away from further downdraughts.

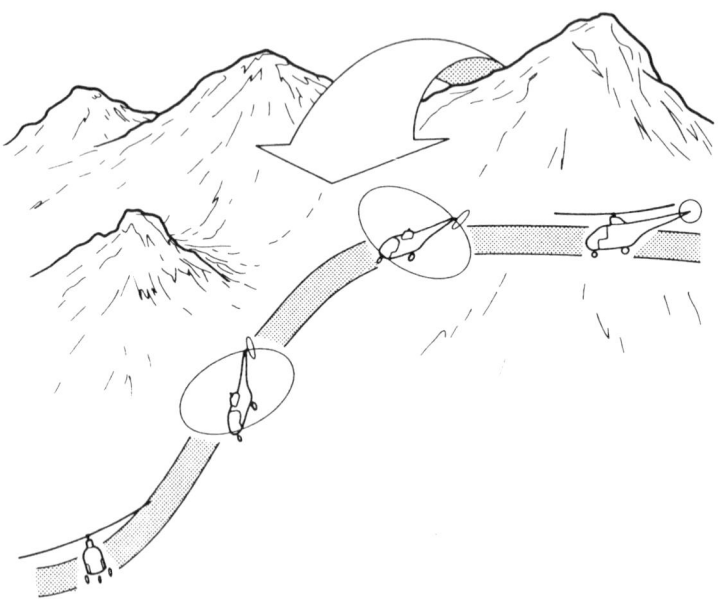

Landing Sites

The main problem with mountain flying is the large variation in terrain, weather, wind, altitude and AUW which can occur from flight to flight. It is therefore unwise and undesirable to insist firmly on a rigid pattern of procedures which lays down speeds, heights and approach paths. Nevertheless, several basic rules must be followed for safe operations.
1. Always ensure an adequate power margin.
2. Establish wind direction and behaviour.
3. Conduct a proper reconnaissance before any landing.
4. Select sound escape routes.
5. Fly a safe circuit with a constant angle of approach.

The following techniques should provide a framework for any helicopter pilot to make safe approaches, landings and take-offs to various types of features and under most conditions.

POWER MARGIN

It is essential to have sufficient power available to carry out a particular approach and to know when you are close to those power limits. Turbulence and downdraughts will rapidly absorb power, and may require power corrections that easily exceed the power available. It is therefore vital that a power check is carried out in the vicinity of the landing site **before** any landing is attempted.

At a safe height, fly straight and level into the wind at the speed which gives the best rate of climb for the helicopter and note the **power required**. Now apply **maximum power available**. The difference between the two readings is the **power margin**. The power margin dictates what type of landing, if any, can be carried out, or whether there is sufficient power available to establish a hover should a landing not be possible.

On take-off, a slightly lower hover than normal should be established and the power required noted. Apply maximum power available, ensuring that maximum permitted RPM are maintained. Again the difference between the two readings is the power margin which determines the types of take-off available to you.

WIND DIRECTION AND BEHAVIOUR

Before approaching a specific mountain feature, the pilot will already be aware of the wind conditions in the general area. However, the wind affecting the area of the landing site may well be influenced by other factors. It is important that this 'local' wind is determined before any approach and landing. Two common methods are outlined below.

Constant Airspeed/Constant Power

This method has limited application, but may be useful on pinnacles and ridges.

An orbit of the feature is carried out at touchdown height at constant airspeed, power and angle of bank. On the updraughting side the helicopter will gain height and on the downdraughting side it will lose height. If very strong up- or downdraughts are evident, power adjustment may be necessary to maintain a safe altitude.

The position of the demarcation line and the breadth of the turbulent segment to the lee of the feature should also be ascertained. The lighter the wind the closer to the feature the orbit must be flown and at a lower airspeed. On a pinnacle an escape route to the outside is always open.

On a ridge, this method can be used by conducting a straight, level run-up each side of the ridge at a constant speed and power. This will show the updraughting on one side and the downdraughting on the other, but does not pinpoint the actual wind direction to the extent that a pinnacle does.

Cloverleaf Pattern

A level run is made at about 50 feet above the feature (higher if there is danger of downdraughts) at a constant airspeed across the landing site on a selected heading. Drift will be experienced to port or starboard unless by chance, a direct into- or downwind run is chosen. Turn through 270° in the direction of the drift, then make a further run across the site at right angles to the previous run. The

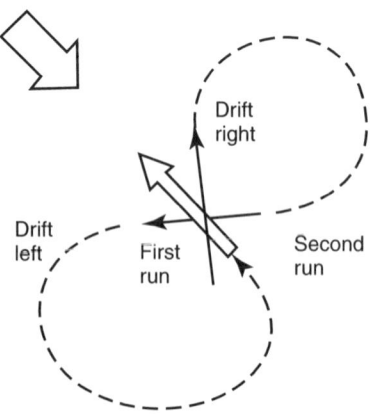

drift experienced on this run should place the wind direction within a 90° quadrant. Next, make a wide turn again in the direction of the drift to bisect the quadrant so as to track over the landing site as nearly into wind as possible. This procedure can be continued as required until an accurate wind direction has been established.

THE RECONNAISSANCE

A carefully executed reconnaissance of the site is an important pre-requisite to a safe landing and take-off. Remember, do not commit yourself to a landing before determining that a safe take-off can be made.

The reconnaissance is split into two phases:

The High Reconnaissance (general reconnaissance)

The height at which this is flown depends on the position of the landing point relative to the ground around it, the wind strength and direction, and the turbulence. Height references in the vicinity of the landing site may be few and constant reference should be made to the altimeter to prevent descending below the level of the landing point.

The pattern to be flown while carrying out the reconnaissance is dictated mainly by the position of the landing point relative to the ground around it. The basic pattern shown below can be modified to meet the requirements of any given situation.

This pattern should be flown as many times as necessary to achieve an initial assessment of the following points:

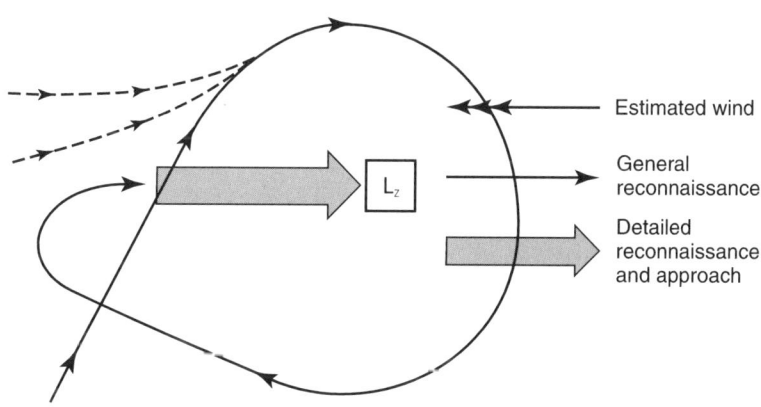

a) The general feature wind velocity, noting any local feature which may cause turbulence or up-/downdraughts.
b) The approximate height of the landing area. This is important, as subsequent height calculations will be based on this figure. From a distance, optical illusions can create the impression that the feature is above you when, from the altimeter, you know that you are higher than the feature.
c) Possible landing points. These should be near the upwind edge of the feature and clear of obstructions.
d) Provisional approach and take-off paths, bearing in mind the power margin, wind behaviour and obstructions.
e) Escape routes, ideally one each side of the approach path within 45° of the approach heading. These must be downslope, preferably towards updraughting air.
f) Plan the low reconnaissance and circuit pattern.

The Low Reconnaissance (detailed reconnaissance)

The aim of the low reconnaissance is to confirm or modify the observations and decisions made on the high reconnaissance, as well as to select a definite landing point. Any changes made should only be minor. Major changes will require a complete reassessment, including a further high reconnaissance.

The following points must be carefully established:
a) The wind velocity and behaviour, up-/downdraughts, turbulence and the angle of the demarcation line.
b) The best approach path.
c) The best landing point. Consider size, shape, surface, slope and surrounds. Be wary of slopes. It is not unusual to find a steep slope on a site judged to be level.
d) Alternative landing points.
e) Escape routes.

The low reconnaissance may take several circuits, but when you have confirmed your approach plan you will be ready to fly the final circuit.

The Circuit

The circuit leads on naturally from the high and low reconnaissances. Ideally it should be flown as a race-track pattern at about 200 feet above the landing site, aligned with the approach track. Both height and shape will be dictated by terrain and wind behaviour. An escape route should be kept available at all times if possible. Carry out the pre-landing checks and then set the helicopter up on the final approach heading.

Approaches and Take-Offs

Whenever possible, a constant angle-of-approach technique should be used. Plan to use the minimum power required technique and continue the approach to the hover. The landing point will often be outlined against other features when you are flying down the approach path. If the landing point is held stationary against the background, the angle of approach will remain constant.

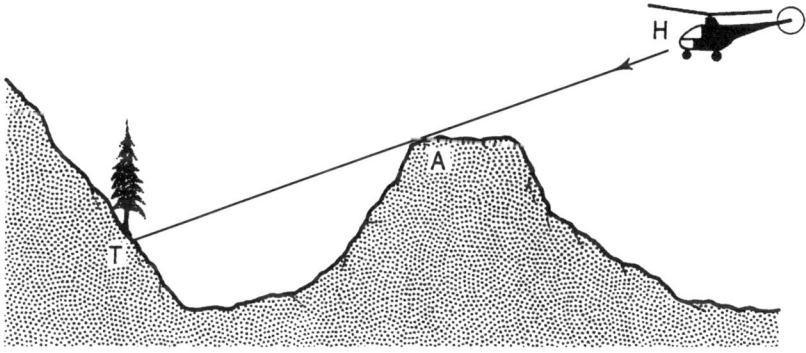

In the diagram above, the pilot is approaching to land at **A**. When **HAT** is constant, the angle of approach is steady.

If the helicopter sinks below the desired angle, the landing point will move up against the background.

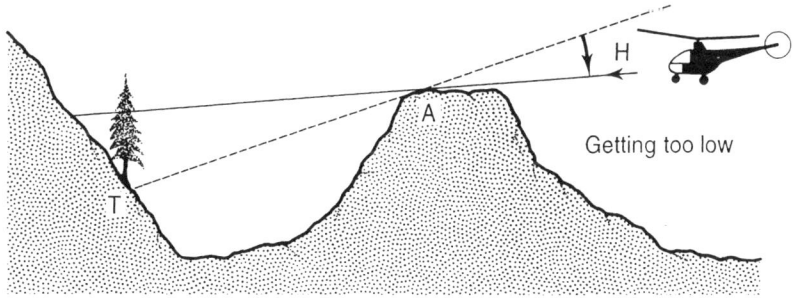

Similarly, if the helicopter goes above the desired angle of approach, the landing point will appear to move down against the background.

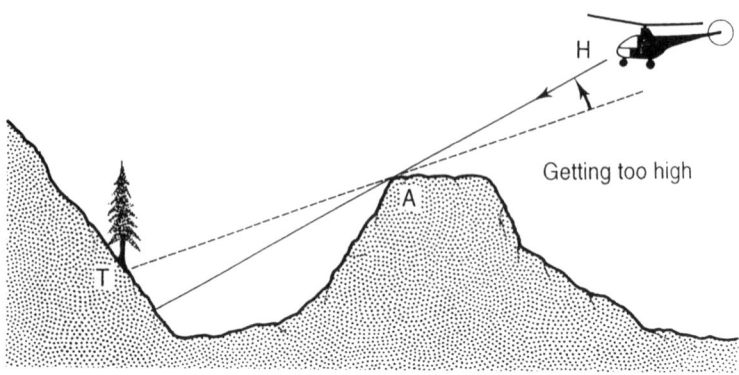

APPROACH SPEED

The initial approach speed will vary according to the wind strength and distance from the landing point. Ideally it should be around 30 kts + wind speed. The normal method of maintaining a constant apparent rate of progress over the ground is not possible because this technique demands a level surface beneath the helicopter. It is therefore very important that approach speeds are controlled by reference to the closing rate, which should appear to remain constant.

With continuous height/speed comparison and careful assessment of the rate of expansion of the landing site through the windscreen, a steady progression towards the landing point should result. Power demand is more progressive than with a more rapid normal approach. Large attitude changes during the latter stages of the approach are to be avoided.

At a certain point during the approach, the speed will reduce to a value where translational lift is lost. The point just before this can be considered as the **decision point**, at which the decision to continue or overshoot is made. If adequate control and power margins exist at the decision point, and turbulence is acceptable, the approach can be continued to the landing point.

THE LANDING

Since it is virtually impossible to judge with any degree of certainty whether or not the landing site is level, the first approach should be to the hover. The landing should be made using the sloping-ground techniques.

THE TAKE-OFF

Before lifting off into the hover, carry out the pre-take-off checks. Then consider the possible take-off paths. Unless conditions have changed significantly, plan to use the routes selected during the pre-landing reconnaissance.

Lift off into the hover, point the helicopter on to the take-off heading and carry out a power margin check. This will determine the type of transition to be employed. Always try to use the minimum power required technique for the transition. From a low hover, apply power as necessary for the transition. If the choice of take-off path allows it, dive or move down slope to gain climbing speed as quickly as possible.

Obviously an up-valley transition is the worst possible case, as the helicopter must be capable of climbing and accelerating before it is possible to turn towards the valley entrance. The requirement to accelerate, climb and turn in downdraughts and turbulence requires a very large power margin and may be quite hazardous.

Flying along Slopes

If flight along the side of a slope becomes necessary, the helicopter should be positioned so as to obtain a straight flight path and also to gain maximum benefit from ascending air.

When joining the slope it should be approached at an angle not exceeding 45°. This angle should be reduced progressively as wind strength increases.

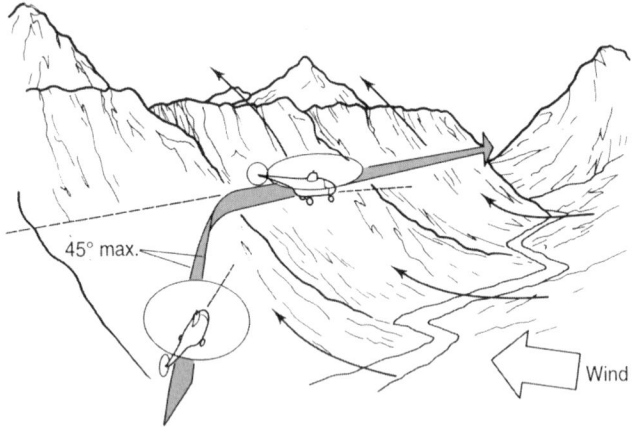

While flying along a slope beware of becoming mesmerised by it, as there could be a danger of flying into any protruding ground.

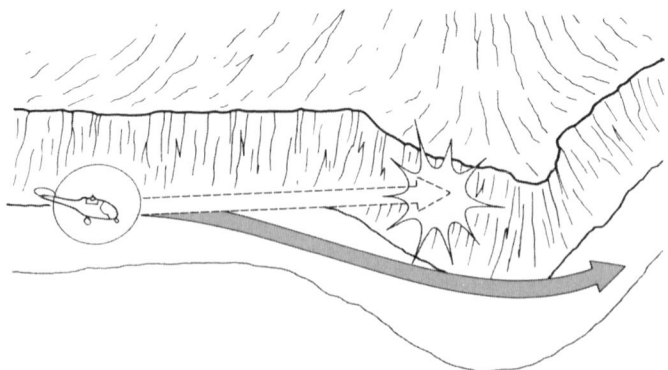

When you need to climb over a ridge line you should take advantage of updraughts to reduce time spent in the climb. When approaching the mountainside in search of maximum updraught you should not do so by facing into the mountain, but by placing the helicopter on a converging course to the line of the ridge. If you need to gain height in a given area, you should do so in a series of figure-eight turns and not by a spiral climb.

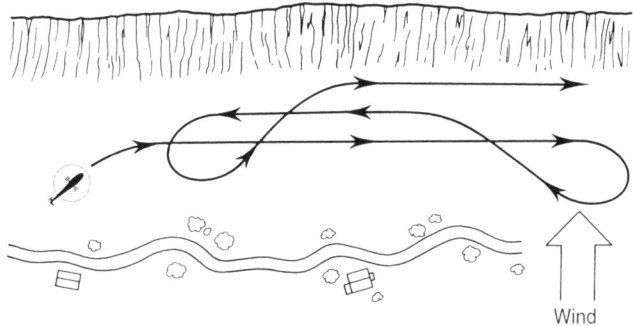

Never attempt to take advantage of the updraught which may be found close to the far side of the ridge relative to the wind, as the turbulence on that side can be very dangerous.

LANDING SITES ON SLOPES

The landing site can be either on the windward or lee side of a hill. Normally the most favourable is that situated on the windward side. The site on the lee side presents problems which you are likely to accept only under emergency conditions.

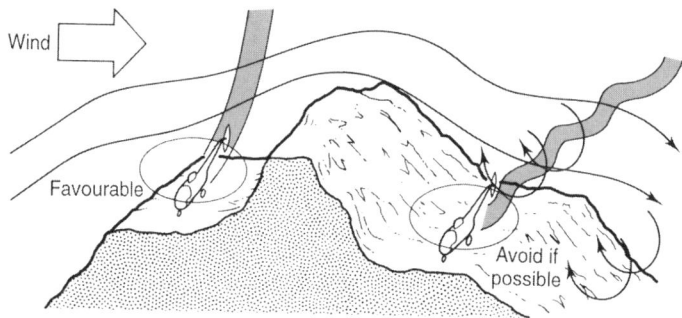

RECONNAISSANCE OF SLOPE SITES

Little problem is involved in the reconnaissance of the site on the windward slope. However, on the lee side, owing to turbulence and downdraughts, the wind may have no firm direction. Once the direction of approach is established, the selection of approach reference points will be of great assistance.

APPROACHES TO THE SLOPE

Aim to approach the landing site with the wind in the front sector. **Do not approach face-on to the slope.** Make the approach path angle such that an escape can be made immediately if necessary.

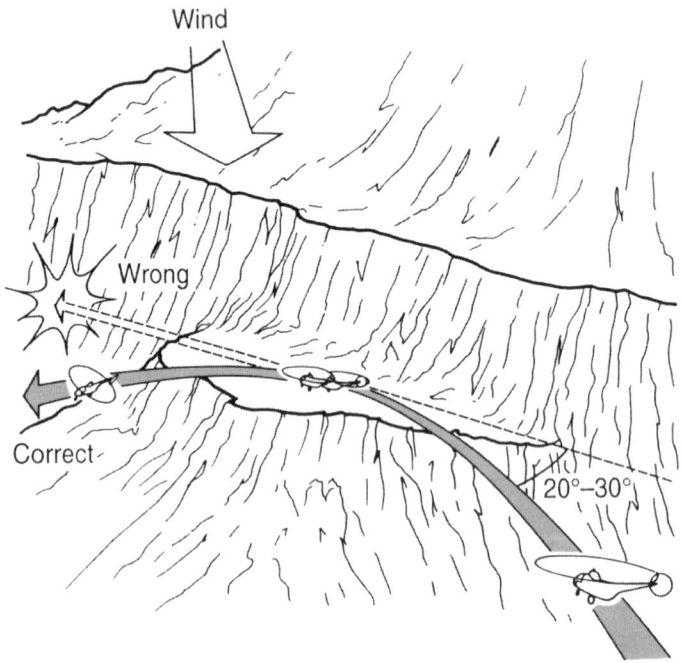

INLAND EMPIRE RENTAL SERVICES

"Your Home Rental Specialist"

909.931.9630 • 909.982.9384
130-H South Mountain Ave., Upland, CA 91786
ierentals@inbox.com

Crests and Pinnacles

Wind at 90° to a regular shaped ridge will, in the main, produce updraughts on the windward side and downdraughts and turbulence on the lee side.

CROSSING A CREST LINE

The passage of a crest line should always be made much higher than the height of the crest itself. The amount of height in hand over the crest will vary with the conditions prevailing, but even in relatively good conditions, **never try to 'scrape' over a crest line**.

When approaching a crest line, gain clearance height and approach at an angle not exceeding 45°. Once the crest has been crossed, the angle should be increased so that you are flying away from the crest and its associated turbulence as quickly as possible.

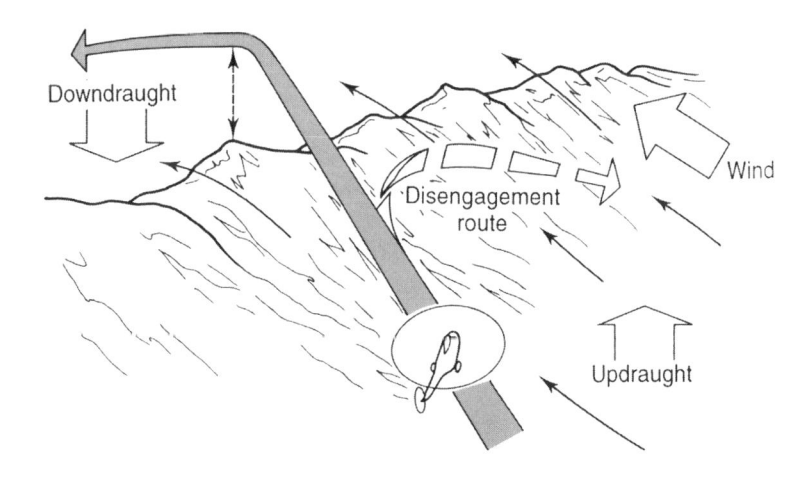

FLIGHT OVER CRESTS FROM THE WINDWARD SIDE

The gain in altitude required to cross the crest can be made on the lifting slope but care must be taken that the increased ground speed which becomes apparent as you near the crest, due to flying downwind, does not lead you to reduce airspeed. **Watch your ASI.** If you are unable to cross on the first approach, turn and climb on the lifting slope. Anticipate the increase in wind as the crest line is crossed and the area of downdraughts beyond it.

FLIGHT OVER CRESTS FROM THE LEE SIDE

It is not possible to climb on a lee slope, so you must start your climb early and gain altitude before the area of downdraughts and turbulence is encountered. Cross the crest with an even greater margin of height to avoid being caught by downdraughts. **Do not try and 'scrape' over the crest, but turn away in good time if you think you have insufficient altitude in hand.**

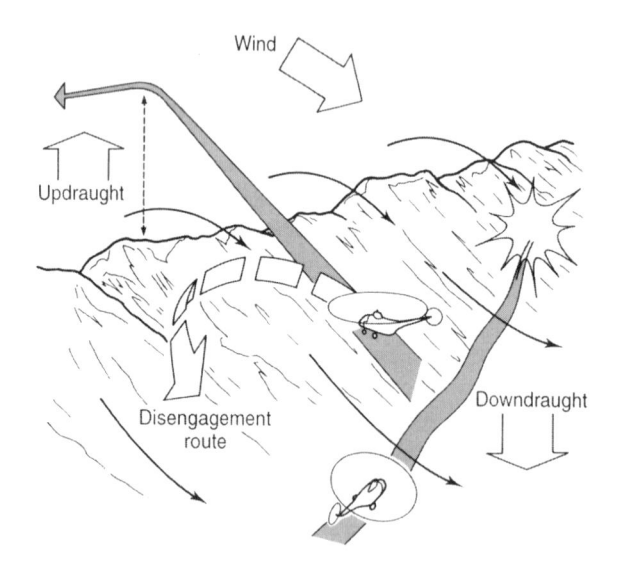

APPROACHES TO CRESTS AND PEAKS

No Wind The way you fly your reconnaissance, circuit and approach will be dictated by the ground. The approach will vary in angle from normal to flat.

Strong Wind This is always associated with turbulence and it is wind and turbulence that dictate the way that the reconnaissance circuit and approach are flown. The approach angle will vary from normal to steep. An approach on to a peak is made by either a straight approach with the wind in the front sector, or by a descending turn into the wind.

The way a crest is approached is dictated by the way the wind is blowing relative to the line of the crest. When the wind is blowing along a crest line, approach the crest obliquely, aiming to land on its forward end.

Approach onto a peak

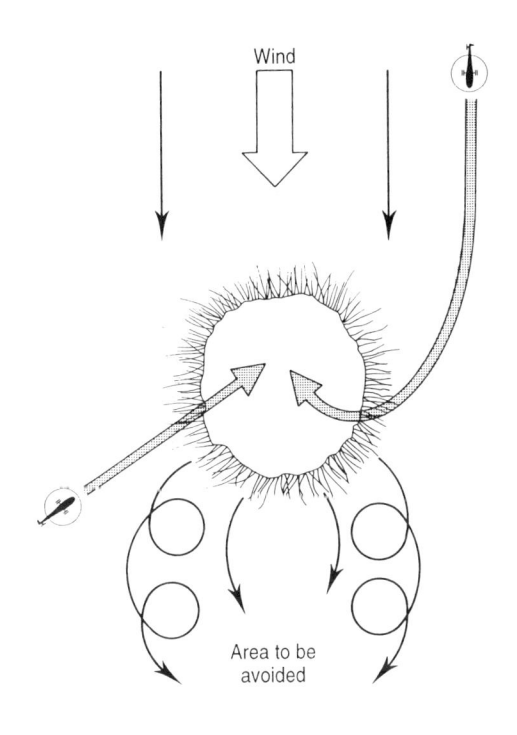

Wind

Area to be avoided

Approaching a crest with wind blowing along it

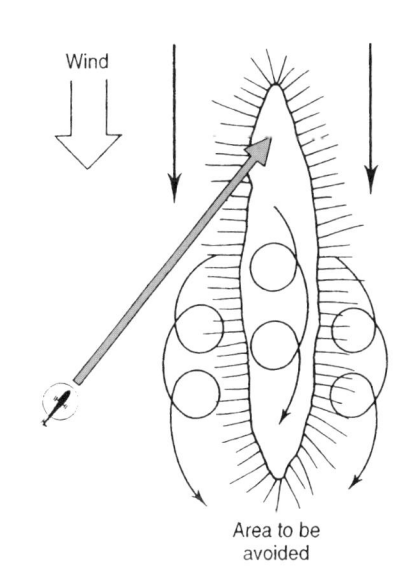

Wind

Area to be avoided

When the wind is blowing over a crest line, make the approach along the line of the crest and land on its forward end.

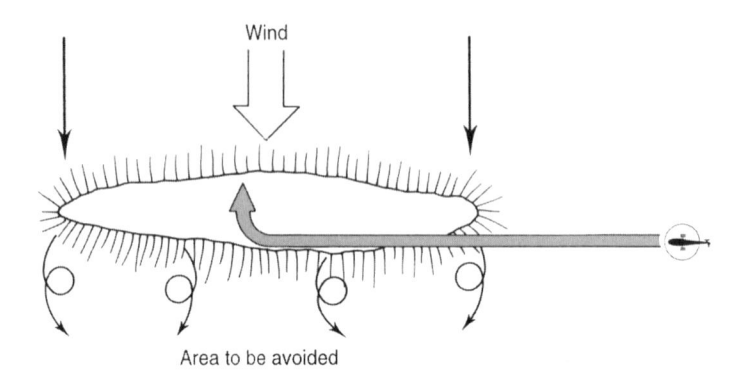

Area to be avoided

TAKE-OFFS

The type of take-off to be aimed for is the one that gives you the best power margin. If the power margin is less than that required for a normal take-off, then providing the terrain, obstacles and helicopter type allow it, a jump take-off can be effected.

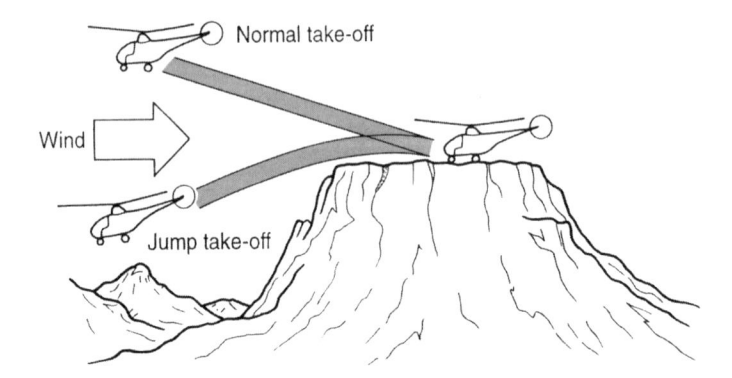

Flight in and along Valleys

Flight along a narrow valley may bring together a number of unfavourable flight conditions:
The absence of any normal horizon.
The accentuation of funnel effect and, if the valley is climbing, that of slope also.
A limitation of action available to the pilot in the event of an emergency.
Natural and artificial obstacles, such as HT cables, which, when slung across a valley, become almost invisible.

When possible, always fly down a valley towards its exit and low ground. When flying up a valley there is always the danger of flying past the point at which a 180° turn is possible. Avoid flying along the centre of a valley. Try and fly on the 'lifting' side.

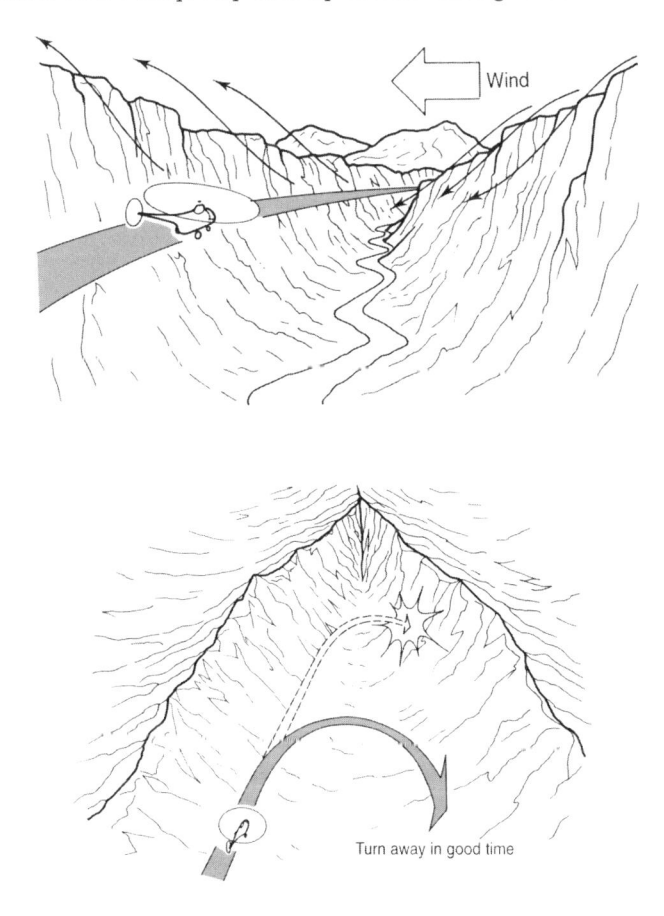

Turn away in good time

When flying up a valley, do not pass the last point at which a 180° turn is possible unless you know that an exit exists beyond. Fly down rather than up a valley whenever possible. Pay frequent reference to flight instruments, especially the ASI, in order to maintain correct and safe flight conditions. Always turn away in good time, and make the turn away from the nearest slope.

LANDING SITES

Landing sites in the bottoms of valleys often have difficult access and frequently leave no escape route open once an approach is started. For this reason it is necessary to ensure that a safe reserve of power is available before committing yourself to an approach. If the valley is at altitude, the power margin will be reduced and you should avoid flying close to the ground downwind in these conditions.

RECONNAISSANCE

Owing to the limits of manoeuvre, the reconnaissance of a landing site in a deep valley is more difficult than normal and therefore it should always be approached with forethought and caution. During the reconnaissance special attention should be paid to wind direction, difficulties of access and the route in and out. Note also any obstacles in the area of the landing site and estimate their effect on take-off.

APPROACHES AND TAKE-OFFS

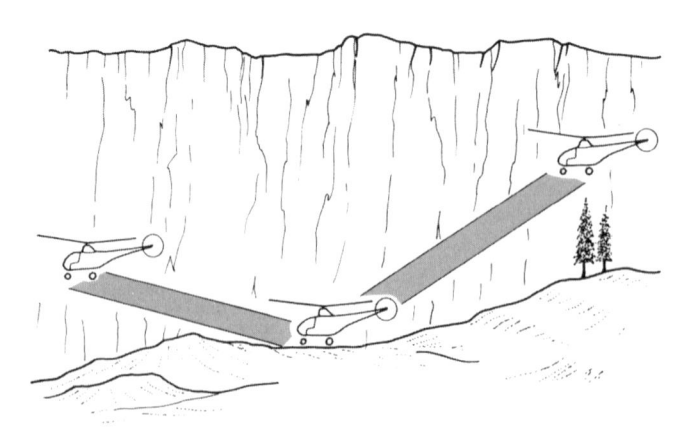

If the wind is following the axis of the valley, the approach and take-off should be made into the wind. In conditions of no wind or crosswinds, the shape of the ground will dictate the direction of approach and take-off. Always try to approach and take off down the slope.

Use the sight picture technique to avoid obstacles on the approach and to be in a position to convert height to speed should an overshoot become necessary.

Flights through a Col

A col forms a 'double' venturi and the wind effects are likely to be greater than those found elsewhere in the mountains. Even when the wind is generally light there will often be a current of air moving through a col. Any rocky outcrops should be avoided as they will give rise to violent turbulences.

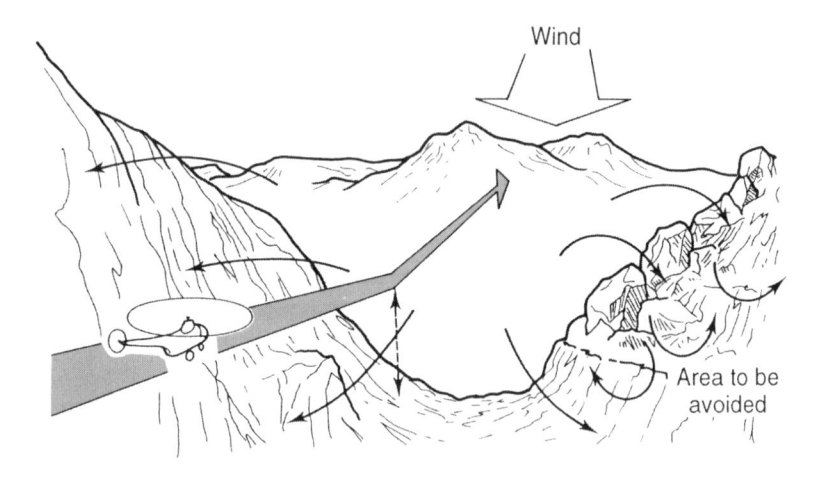

The passage of a col combines all the techniques of slope flying, flight through a valley and the passage of a crest. Always approach with a good margin of height, and always approach along one slope and never fly along the axis of the col.

Note the point beyond which a 180° turn becomes impossible and do not hesitate to turn back before this point is reached if you have the slightest doubt about making a safe passage through the col. Avoid flying close over sharp features.

Effects of Sun and Shadow

The effect of the sun in the mountains is to create a marked temperature difference between those slopes in sunlight and those in shadow. This gives rise to up- and downdraughts. A further effect is to make the appreciation of angles and distances more difficult.

In selecting the approach to any landing site, sun and shadow effects should always be taken into consideration, as well as the wind. When the landing point is in shadow avoid flying in the sun. Try to make the whole of the approach in the shade.

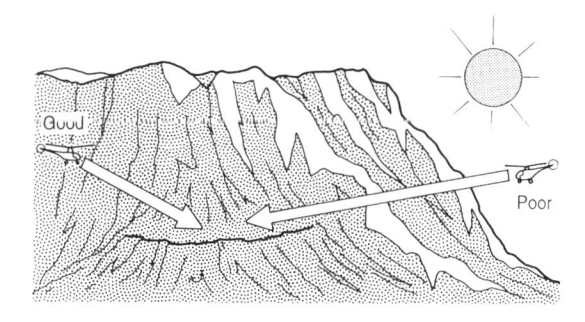

When the landing point is in the sun the conditions of observation are better. In this case part of the approach may be made in shadow if necessary, but it is always better to make the whole of the approach in the sun if possible.

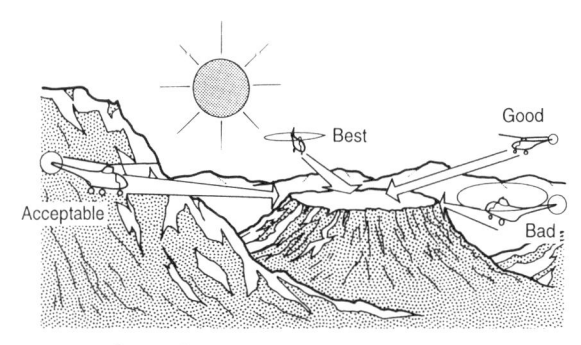

In the sun, good conditions of observation are obtained with the sun at 90° to the line of approach. The best conditions, however, will be obtained when the sun is behind the helicopter. Always try and avoid the glare which attends the passage from shadow to sunshine and avoid making your approach into sun when it is low on the horizon.

Common Faults

The most common faults shown by helicopter pilots in the early stages of mountain flying are:
Climbing towards high ground and descending towards low ground.
Losing airspeed when flying towards high ground and gaining airspeed when flying towards low ground.
Large variations of height and speed in the circuit owing to rapid changes in ground clearance.
Slow, flat approaches towards the landing point on rising ground owing to false visual clues.
Failure to appreciate the slope of landing sites.
Failure to monitor flight instruments sufficiently.
Apprehension, leading to tenseness on the controls.

Remember
Always use maximum rotor RPM.
Avoid areas where downdraughts are likely to be found.
Anticipate increased wind strength near cols, crests, valleys and peaks.
When flying close to the ground, reduce to climb speed.
Always have a good escape route.

ENJOY YOUR MOUNTAIN FLYING SAFELY

Part Two

Advanced Flying Techniques

Helicopter Weight and Balance

Readers should have learned the basic principles of weight and balance, and the importance of understanding their helicopter's loading limitations, during their primary flight training. Almost every aspect of helicopter performance is influenced by weight. An overloaded helicopter requires more power for all phases of flight, has a shorter range, reduced cruising speed and could possibly exceed its control limits.

To understand how the weight of a helicopter determines the loads imposed on it during flight, you should first refresh your knowledge of the term **Load Factor**. When we discuss stresses on the helicopter, then the load factor is the ratio of **Actual Load** to **Helicopter Weight**. It is determined by dividing the actual load being applied by the total weight of the helicopter. Load factors are normally expressed in 'Gs'.

A 'G' is equal to the force of gravity or the actual weight of an object at rest. For example, a helicopter has a load factor of one 'G' when at rest on the ground. It also experiences one 'G' when in a steady climb or flying straight and level in smooth air.

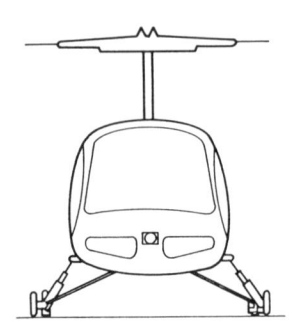

When you are flying in gusting conditions the loads imposed are dependent on your airspeed. Flying through turbulence at high speed causes the rotor blades to be subjected to high load factors. Because of this you should always reduce speed when encountering turbulent conditions.

When you enter a steep co-ordinated turn and reach 60° of bank, your helicopter is being subjected to a load factor of two. This means the rotor blades are lifting double the weight experienced in straight and level flight.

If the helicopter weight is 2,000 lb, the effective weight in a 60° bank turn is 4,000 lb.

60° banked turn

2 Gs force
(4,000 lb)

(Helicopter weighs 2,000 lb)

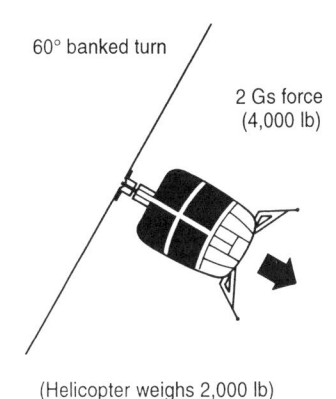

All the information for the proper loading of your helicopter will be found in the Flight Manual. To ensure that these operating limitations are not exceeded, it will be necessary for you to calculate the helicopter's total weight at any particular time.

The following are a reminder of the most commonly used terms:
Standard Empty Weight The weight of the helicopter and all its basic equipment including unusable fuel, full oil and full operating fluids.
Basic Empty Weight Standard Empty Weight plus installed optional equipment.
Maximum All-Up Weight (MAUW) The maximum permitted total weight of the helicopter.
Maximum Take-Off Weight Maximum permitted weight at which the helicopter may take-off in the ambient conditions.
Maximum Operating Weight The maximum weight permitted for operations after take-off, e.g. external load lifting.
Useful Load The difference between Take-Off Weight and Basic Empty Weight.
Payload The weight of crew, passengers, baggage, etc.
Usable Fuel Fuel available for flight planning.
Unusable Fuel The fuel remaining after an engine run-out test.

The basic empty weight of your helicopter can be found in the Weight and Balance Schedule. This is either included in the Flight Manual or published separately as part of the helicopter's documentation. The total weight can then easily be checked by adding to it the weight of fuel carried, the weight of pilot and passengers, and the weight of any baggage/cargo.

Since fuel weighs approximately 7.2 lb per Imperial gallon, (6 lb/US gallon), the total fuel weight is easily calculated by multiplying the number of gallons of fuel on board by 7.2. Be careful of mixed units such as litres/kgs/US gallons.

1 kg = 2.205 lb	1 lb = 0.454 kg
1 Imp gal = 4.546 litres	1 litre = 0.22 Imp gal
1 US gal = 3.785 litres	1 litre = 0.264 US gal
1 Imp gal = 1.205 US gal	1 US gal = 0.83 Imp gal

If you have any doubts over passenger weights, be safe and weigh them. Actual cargo and baggage weights should always be used. An example of a weight check is:

Basic empty weight	1,550 lb
Pilot	180 lb
Passenger	180 lb
Fuel (40 US Gal)	240 lb
Baggage	50 lb
	2,200 lb

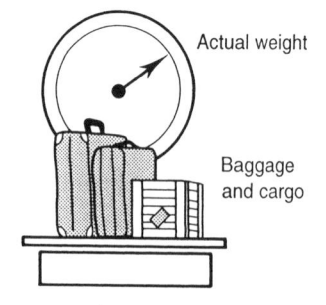

Assuming that the helicopter has a permitted MAUW of 2,350 lb, its weight of 2,200 lb is well within its operating limitations.

Remember it is *not* always possible to fill all the seats and carry full fuel and baggage and remain within the approved limits for your helicopter. You may have to reduce the number of passengers or the baggage or fuel load (or possibly a combination of all three) to stay legal.

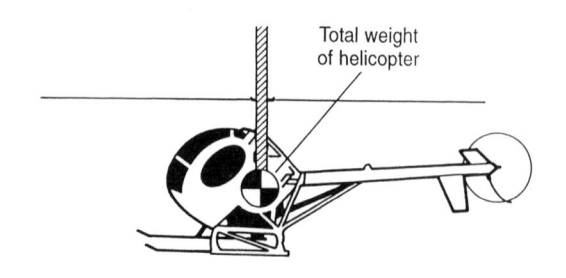

In addition to checking weight, you must also know that your helicopter is correctly balanced within its approved limits. The balance condition of your helicopter can be determined by locating its **Centre of Gravity** (C of G). This is an imaginary point where the helicopter would balance if suspended.

The C of G of a helicopter is normally located very near to the main rotor mast. Forward and aft limits are laid down by the manufacturer and established during certification flight testing. These are the extreme C of G positions at which the longitudinal stability of your helicopter can be controlled. If you operate outside these limits you will be flying in an area where the helicopter's handling has not been checked, or is unsatisfactory. Therefore, you **must not** fly your helicopter outside its permitted limits.

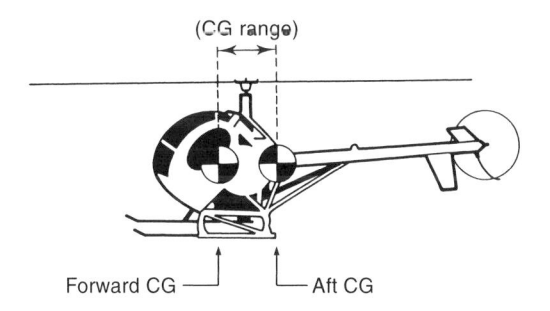

The C of G and limits are usually specified in inches from a **reference datum**. This is an imaginary point from which all horizontal distances are measured for balance purposes. There is no fixed rule as to the location of the datum, it is established by the manufacturer. Most light helicopters have their datum forward of the nose.

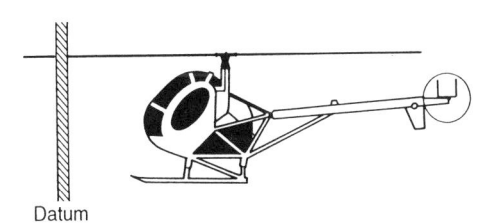

The **Lateral C of G reference datum**, however, is normally located through the centre of the helicopter. As long as you maintain the C of G within the permitted limits for your helicopter you will have adequate cyclic control in all manoeuvres.

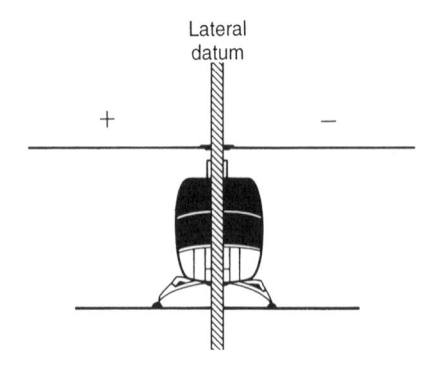

An undesirable C of G forward of the limits can occur in most light helicopters when a heavy pilot and passengers are combined with a light fuel load. The flight may begin with the C of G within limits but, as the fuel burns off, the C of G will move forward and could exceed the forward limit. This forward C of G condition will be evident as you lift off to the hover. The helicopter will have a nose-down attitude and will require more than normal aft cyclic pressure.

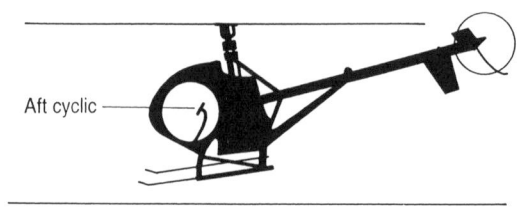

There could also be insufficient cyclic control to decelerate and stop. In extreme cases during autorotation, cyclic control could be restricted enough to prevent a proper flare before landing.

Hovering in a strong wind can easily mask a forward C of G position. Always get into the habit of noting cyclic position and wind strength every time you lift off to the hover.

Exceeding the aft C of G limits is recognisable by the tail-low attitude and the need for more than normal forward cyclic when you lift off to the hover.

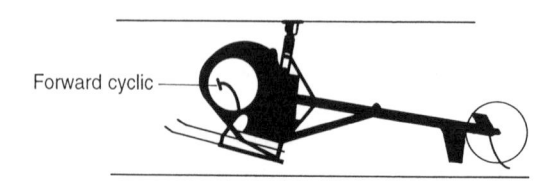

This forward cyclic will be increased as the wind velocity increases. Another indication of an aft C of G is the inability to reach the higher airspeeds at which you normally fly.

When you measure the distance from the datum to the weight you are measuring the **arm**.

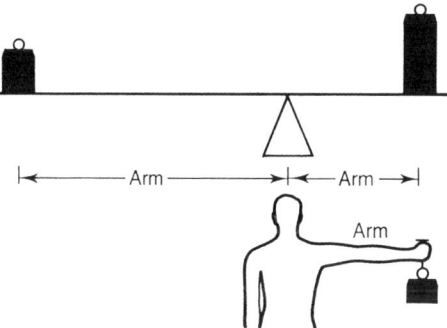

The tendency for an object to rotate is equal to its weight multiplied by its distance (arm) from the fulcrum. This product is called the **moment** and is usually stated in **pound-inches**. For example, a 10 lb weight supported from a 24 in arm would have a moment of 240 lb/in.

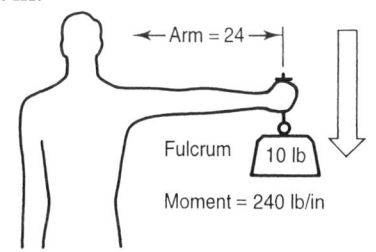

The reference datum of the helicopter can be likened to the fulcrum and the C of G to the balance point.

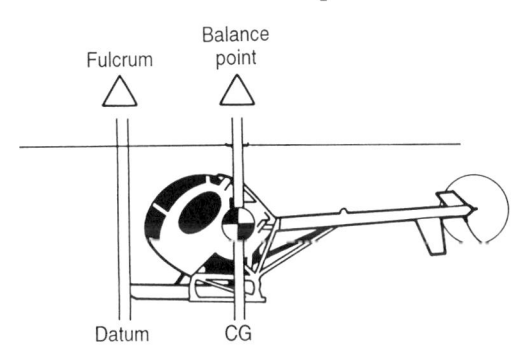

By convention, all arms located to the left of the datum are labelled **minus** and all arms to the right **plus**.

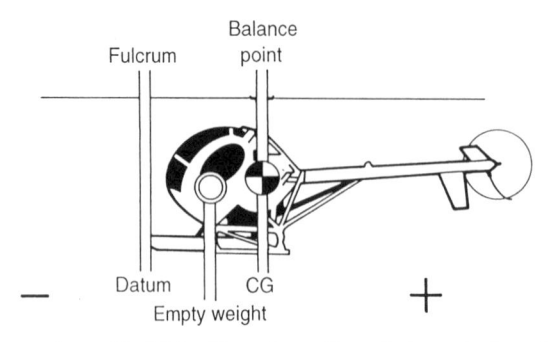

```
                    Balance
         Fulcrum    point


           ⊖  ⊙
      —    Datum    CG         +
           Empty weight
```

On many modern light helicopters the datum is located 100 in forward of the main rotor mast centre line. This means, therefore, that all items will have **positive** arms.

WEIGHT AND BALANCE CALCULATION

Since weight and balance is so critical to the safe operation of your helicopter, it is important that you understand how to check its condition for any loading arrangement. If you had to weigh and measure every item from the datum each time you needed to computate the C of G, it would be very time consuming indeed. To simplify the task, the manufacturer includes tables and graphs in the helicopter's operating manual for easy reference.

To calculate the C of G, you should first list the basic empty weight, pilot, fuel, passengers, baggage, etc, together with their respective weights and arms. Then multiply the weights and arms together to find the moment of each item. (The helicopter's weight schedule should list the basic empty weight together with its moment.) Add all the weights together to get the total weight. Add all the moments to find the total moment. Divide the total moment by the total weight to obtain the C of G position.

Compare the total weight to the maximum permitted all-up weight and the C of G location with the certificated forward and aft limits. If there are any discrepancies you will have to adjust the loading as necessary to keep your helicopter within its approved limits.

Sample loading calculation

Suppose we have the following information in the helicopter's operating manual:
The longitudinal C of G limits are shown to be variable with gross weight from 92 in to 100 in aft of the datum, and the lateral C of G

Longitudinal CG

[Diagram: helicopter side view with stations 64.0, 93.446, 135.0 (forward weighing station), 96.0, 119.75, 100.0 C rotor hub, 320.0 aft weighing station]

[Chart: Longitudinal CG — Gross weight (lb) vs Longitudinal CG (inches aft of datum), approved area 92–100, 1,600–2,400 lb]

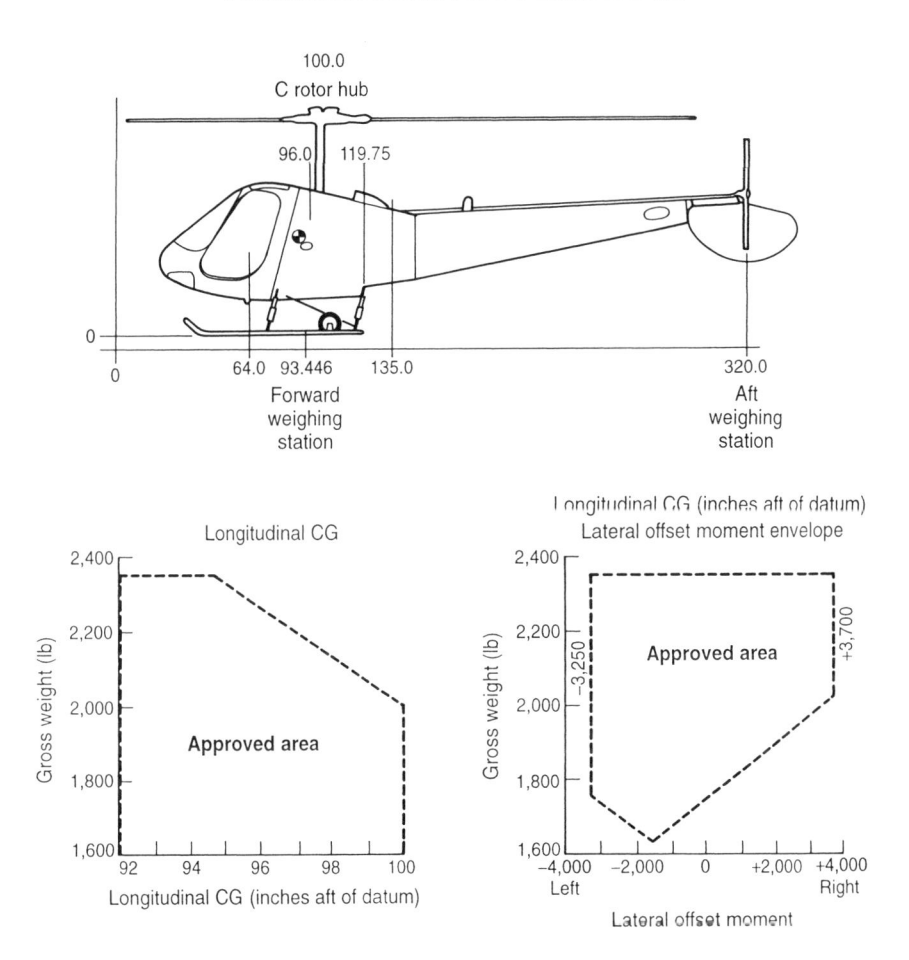

[Chart: Longitudinal CG (inches aft of datum) / Lateral offset moment envelope — Gross weight (lb) vs Lateral offset moment, approved area −3,250 to +3,700, 1,600–2,400 lb]

limits −3,250 in/lb to +3,700 in/lb. The maximum all-up weight is limited to 2,350 lb. If the basic empty weight of the helicopter is 1,495 lb with a moment of 151,593 in/lb, the pilot is 180 lb, passenger 190 lb, baggage 30 lb and fuel load 240 lb, the calculation is as follows:

Item	Weight (lb)	Arm (in)	Moment (in/lb)
Basic Weight	1,495	101.4	151,593.0
Pilot	180	62.0	11,160.0
Passenger	190	62.0	11,780.0
Fuel (40 US gal)	240	96.0	23,040.0
Baggage	30	135.0	4,050.0
Totals	**2,135**		**201,623**

Therefore, C of G = 201,623 divided by 2,135
= 94.44 in aft of datum

The calculated take-off weight of 2,135 lb is below the 2,350 lb MAUW. If you next refer to the Longitudinal C of G Table above and plot a point at 94.44 in against 2,135 lb gross weight, you will see that the C of G position is well within the permitted limits.

The lateral C of G is normally within limits until an external side load is carried. The method of calculation to determine lateral C of G is the same as for longitudinal C of G except for the reference datum position (normally along the helicopter centreline).

You will remember from your aviation law studies that it is a legal requirement for all helicopters to have a valid Certificate of Airworthiness or Permit to Fly. These documents usually specify compliance with the Flight Manual/Pilot's Operating Handbook, which in turn specifies the weight and C of G limits within which the helicopter must be operated. Therefore, if you fail to comply with this legal condition by operating outside any of these limits, your insurance company could reject any claim in the event of a mishap. Be warned!

Underslung Loads

Most helicopters today have the provision for a cargo hook to be fitted to enable them to carry underslung loads. Special instructions for this equipment, together with any weight and C of G limitations, will be found in the Flight Manual/Pilot's Handbook.

In most operations the load will be contained in some form of net. It is very important that you carefully inspect any nets, slings and strops before flight to ensure that they are in good condition and strong enough for the task. It is recommended that the tackle has a breaking strain of not less than four times the weight of the load to be lifted.

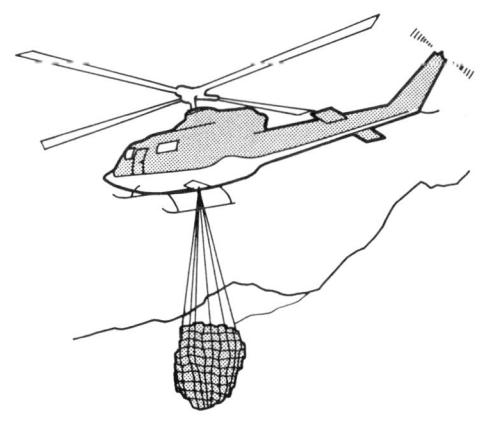

The load itself should be carefully and evenly stacked in the centre of the net, and any sharp edges should be padded to avoid cutting the net. Loads of an uneven shape may spin and cause stress both to the hook and the airframe. As this could affect your flying control of the helicopter, a swivel should be fitted to prevent the strop fouling at the hook or failing through twisting.

As there are many different types of cargo hooks in use today, you must check the type fitted to your helicopter and become familiar with its operation. Check the Flight Manual for any special limitations and pre-flight checks. There should be a placard adjacent to the cargo hook indicating the maximum permissible load for which the installation is approved. In addition to the normal electrical release switch/button, there will be a manual emergency release handle.

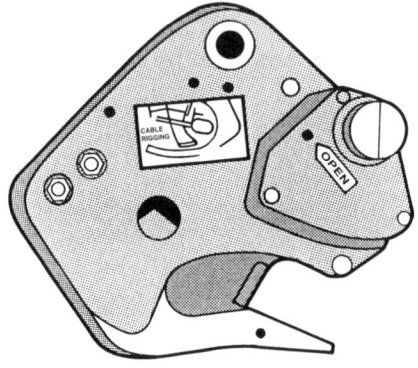

When you hover your helicopter close to the ground it acts as one half of an electrical capacitor, the ground being the other half. During any underslung load operations, all helicopters should be regarded as being charged with static electricity. Any loading or unloading of the hook in the hover should only be undertaken **after** the helicopter has been electrically grounded. Since charging rates can be high, this grounding operation must be maintained throughout.

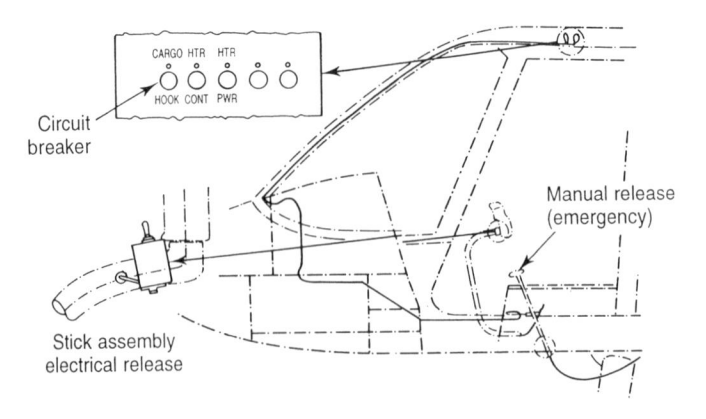

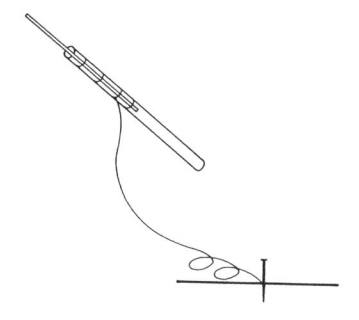

Normally, static electricity is discharged by placing an earthed static discharger firmly against a metal part of the helicopter. A simple discharger can be constructed by connecting an earthing pin (6 inch nail), to about fifteen to twenty feet of insulated copper wire. This wire is then fixed to a conductor (a short length of copper pipe) which is fastened to a length of non-conducting material (a broom handle).

Remember, neither the helicopter nor the load must be touched until they have been earthed or the load has touched the ground.

In addition to the marshaller's hand signals with which you have become familiar, there are some signals special to load lifting.

Move Ahead: Arms repeatedly moved upward and backward, beckoning onward.

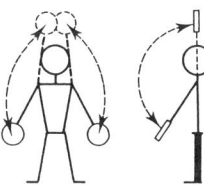

Hover: Arms placed horizontally sideways.

Land: Arms placed down and crossed in front of the body.

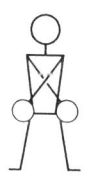

Move Upwards: Arms placed horizontally sideways with the palms up beckoning upwards. The speed of the arm movement indicates the rate of ascent.

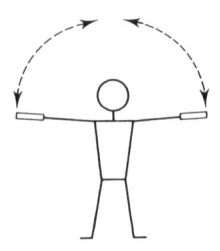

Move Downwards: Arms placed horizontally sideways with palms towards the ground, beckoning. The speed of arm movement indicates the rate of descent.

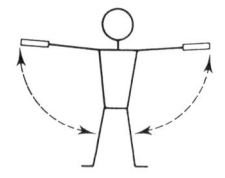

Move Horizontally: Either arm placed horizontally sideways, then the other arm moved in front of the body to that side, in the direction of the movement, indicating that the helicopter should move horizontally to the left or right side, as the case may be.

Move Back: Arms placed down, the palms facing forward, then repeatedly swept up and down to shoulder level.

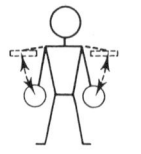

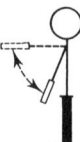

Release the Load: Left arm extended horizontally forward, then right arm making a horizontal slicing movement below left arm.

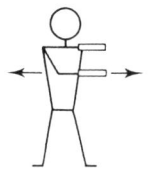

Clear to Go: Right arm fully extended, thumb up, indicating that the helicopter is clear to go.

Only when you have satisfied yourself that the weight of the load to be lifted, the take-off weight and C of G position are all inside approved limits, and that all the ground crew are fully briefed on the procedures to be followed, can you get on with the job of lifting the load.

The simplest method is to land alongside the load so that it can be hooked up with the helicopter on the ground. Then, on the marshaller's signal, you make a gentle lift-off to the hover. Once you are steady you will be directed to position directly above the load. You will then be instructed to climb gently vertically until you feel the load come off the ground.

Alternatively, you can be marshalled over the load and hooked up while maintaining a steady hover. Then, on the marshaller's signal, you initiate a gentle, vertical climb until the load comes off the ground.

You should then assess the power available for the transition and also feel for any load oscillations. Oscillations in the hover are usually caused by the helicopter being incorrectly positioned vertically over the load and causing it to swing on lift-off. They should only last for a short time, and usually damp out quickly if you hold a steady hover.

Do not try to use the cyclic stick to control these oscillations as, more often than not, it will lead you into overcontrolling. If you do have trouble in the hover and it persists, you must do one of two things. Either lower the load back on to the ground or jettison it.

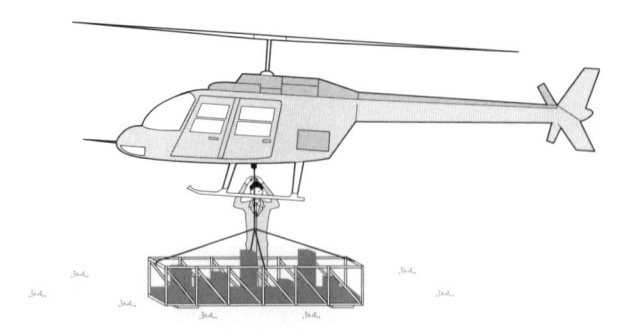

Assuming all is well in the hover and the power available is sufficient, you should then initiate a gentle, smooth, towering-type transition to get you and your load under way.

During the flight, any load oscillations that occur are usually the result of a combination of airspeed and the stability characteristics of the load. Loads of low volume and high density do not normally pose a problem. Large-volume loads of low density and irregular shape are liable to start oscillating at a certain critical airspeed. Your initial accelerations must therefore be made slowly so that you can make a safe approach to this minimum speed if necessary.

If your load starts to oscillate, you should reduce airspeed by at least 10% below this minimum speed. If the load continues to oscillate, a further reduction in airspeed can be tried to damp it out.

Alternatively, a sustained, balanced turn can sometimes be effective in stabilising the load. Should the oscillations continue to the point where you feel it could endanger your control of the helicopter, jettison the load.

On arrival at your destination, having satisfied yourself that you have sufficient power available for a hover outside of ground effect (HOGE), fly a long, slow approach to finish in a high hover. Remember the load is still hanging beneath you. If a marshaller is available, follow his instructions. Otherwise, from a steady hover, gently descend vertically until the load touches the ground. Continue your descent for a few more feet to ensure that the weight change on automatically-opening hooks operates the mechanism; otherwise, release your load with the normal electrical release switch. Then gently move to one side to confirm that the load has released cleanly from the hook. If the load fails to detach using the primary release system, you will have to operate the manual emergency release to clear the hook.

Finally, the Air Navigation Order requires you to have the written permission of the Civil Aviation Authority (CAA) before you can carry any external loads with your helicopter.

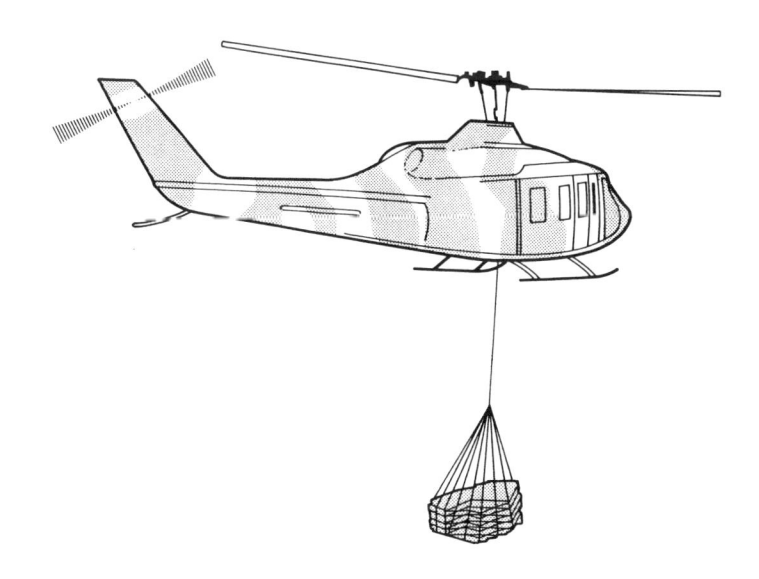

Night Operations

In the *Helicopter Pilot's Manual Volume 1*, under 'Night Flying', the proportional flare path and the techniques required when using it were explained.

Another popular night landing system is the Standard 'T', often known as the NATO 'T'.

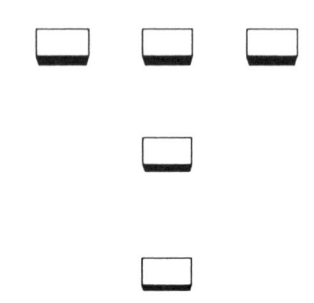

```
    ▭    ▭    ▭

         ▭

         ▭
```

All the lights are positioned 10 m apart and the 'T' is aligned with the prevailing wind. With this layout, after turning on to final approach, you wait until the aspect of the 'T' appears 'normal' before starting your descent. You then maintain the 'T' aspect all the way down to a point just short of the bottom light – the manoeuvre point datum (MPD). As you arrive at this point, keep the helicopter moving gently in the hover taxy and establish a steady hover to one side either at point A or point B.

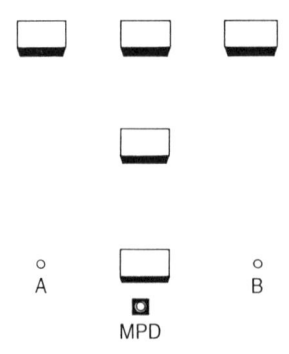

```
    ▭    ▭    ▭

         ▭

    o    ▭    o
    A         B
         ▪
        MPD
```

Quite often, a portable angle of approach indicator (AAI) is used in conjunction with the Standard T. This consists of a metal box containing a battery to power the system, an optical arrangement to project coloured beams of light and a lamp.

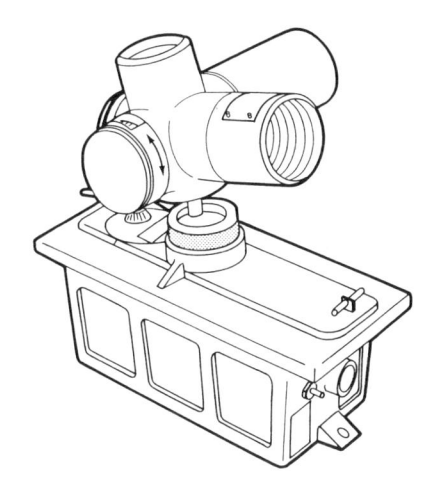

The AAI projects three horizontal beams of light, an **amber** beam to indicate that the approach is too high, a **green** for a correct approach, and a **red** beam to indicate that the pilot is too low. The optical system is designed to allow the operator setting up the equipment to look back up the angle of approach to ensure that the flight path is clear of any obstacles and to provide a means of adjusting the angle if necessary.

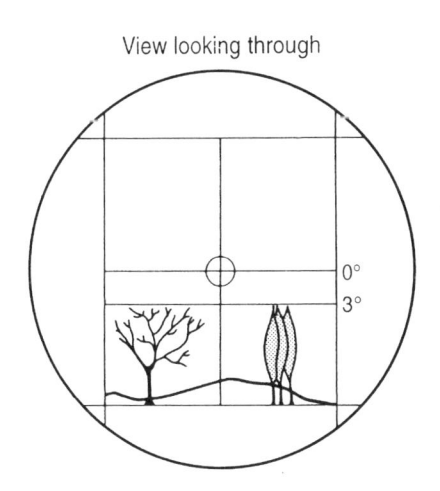

View looking through

0°
3°

When the AAI is to be incorporated into the night landing system, it is usually positioned some 20 m ahead of the top centre light in the 'T'.

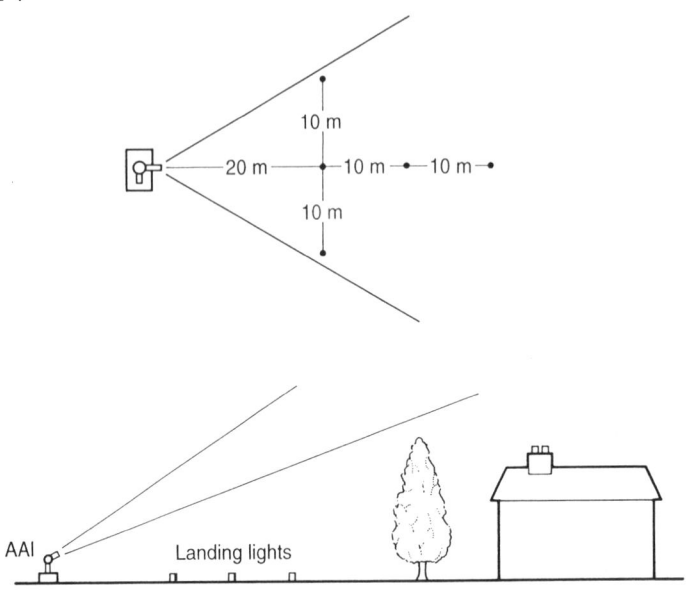

After turning on to final approach you now hold your heading and height until you have both the 'T' aspect and a green light from the AAI. It is important that you continue to fly the 'T' as well as maintaining a 'green' all the way down to the MPD.

The Air Navigation Order states that it is mandatory for helicopters classified under Performance B to carry flares when operating at night. The most popular type is the Schermuly helicopter flare. This is designed primarily as an emergency night landing aid, but can also be used in conjunction with search and rescue operations.

The flare is a parachute type, discharged electrically from a flare mounting. The initial discharge sets off a train which ultimately lights the flare candle and ejects the candle and parachute from the projectile assembly. Usually two separate flares are mounted together in one assembly.

Each flare is about 43 cm long with a diameter of 5.7 cm and weighs approximately 1.58 kg. It is fitted to the mounting with a threaded locking nut. This operation is carried out on the ground so that, once you are airborne, the flares are always ready for use.

When you operate the firing button, a canister is ejected and at about 15 m from the helicopter, opens to allow the flare and parachute to deploy. The flare gives 180,000 candela for about 80 seconds, and falls at between 500 to 600 feet per minute.

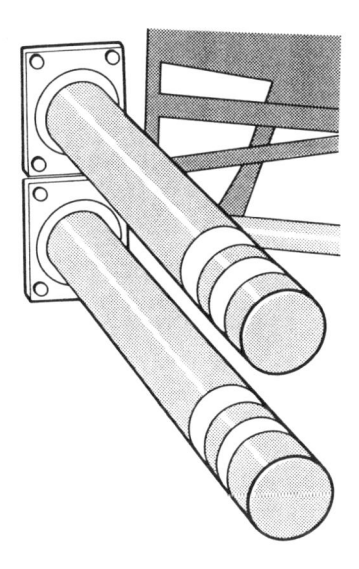

As can be seen from the way the flares operate, they are lethal weapons, so strict safety precautions are essential when they are being used. Whenever flares are installed on your helicopter, regardless of the state of the master switch, the helicopter is to be considered armed and should be positioned so that the flares are directed towards a safe area.

Always handle flares with great care, as they may become unsafe if handled roughly. Flares should only be installed by persons trained or suitably briefed.

You should not set the Flare Armament Switch to the ARMED position until just before take-off. On landing, you should disarm as soon as you clear the flarepath.

If possible, you should have the flares mounted on the side of your helicopter opposite to the one you fly from. This is because in an emergency, especially at night, you tend to turn in the direction of the side from which you fly, to make the forced-landing plan easier. If the flares were fitted to this side as well, you would be turning into the illumination and blinding yourself. Ideally, you would first enter autorotation and then at about 2,500 feet fire off the first flare, at the same time turning away from it. Continue the turn, and after a further 90° or so fire off the second flare. The illumination of the first flare should enable you to select a landing site, and the light from the second flare can be used for the approach and touchdown.

It is easy to be temporarily blinded by the initial ignition, so you must avoid looking towards the flare as you fire it off. It is important that, as you approach the ground for touchdown, the flare(s) are ahead and above you. If they are too low you can easily be dazzled by having to look directly into their light. If they are behind you, you will be landing in your own shadow, which can be most disconcerting and disorientating.

Finally, remember to switch on your landing light as you pass 500 feet AGL, just in case the flares go out.

Another night-flying aid widely used throughout the helicopter world is the Nightsun searchlight. The searchlight consists of a cylindrical housing containing the xenon arc lamp, the reflector, a cooling fan, a focusing motor and the electrical components necessary to ignite the bulb. It produces about 3,800,000 candlepower and can be operated in a 'Spotlight' mode (beam width approximately 4°), through to a 'Floodlight' mode (beam width about 20°).

The complete installation weighs about 25 kg and consists of four parts: **1.** The Gimbal Assembly, **2.** The Junction Box, **3.** The Remote Control Box, **4.** The Searchlight. The gimbal assembly holds the searchlight, and consists of a U-shaped yoke which can be moved in azimuth and elevation by two small DC motors. The junction box is just a small metal container which holds all the relays and connectors for power distribution to the system. The remote control box

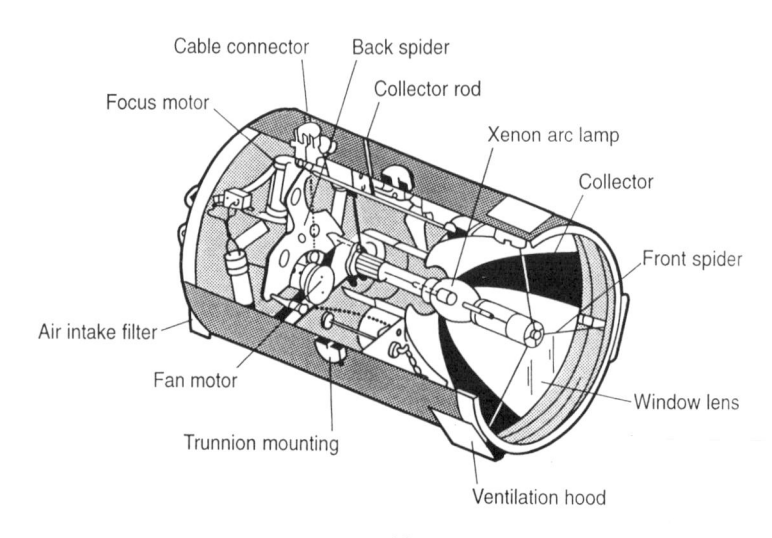

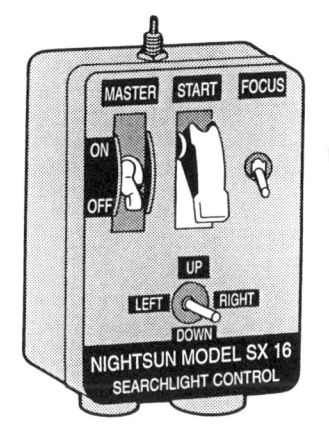

Remote control box — NIGHTSUN MODEL SX 16 SEARCHLIGHT CONTROL

contains the master ON/OFF switch, a START switch for lamp ignition, a lamp FOCUS control and a four-way switch for controlling movement of the searchlight. It can either be panel-mounted or hand-held.

The system requires 28 V DC and 65 Amperes. Accessory power convertors are available for operation from other primary power sources.

Pilot operation of the searchlight is not recommended, not only because of the difficulties of flying the helicopter and controlling the light at the same time, but because you will not be in a position to see the light beam throughout its range of travel.

To operate the searchlight, first turn the master switch on the control box to ON. Press and hold the START switch until the lamp is lit, then release it. (Time to light is approximately two or three seconds.)

The desired beam, i.e. spot or flood, is obtained by operating the FOCUS switch. Note that this is a one-way process, and it is not possible to reverse movement until the limit of the reflector travel has been reached. The travel time from spot to flood and back to spot again is about five or six seconds. The four-way switch can now be used to direct the light in azimuth and elevation. Be careful that the beam is not directed in such a way that light will be reflected back into the cockpit. This can easily happen if the beam strikes the rotor disc or the undercarriage structure.

The light can be extinguished by switching the control box master switch to OFF and then back ON again to operate the cooling fan. No attempt should be made to re-ignite the lamp for at least three minutes after switching it off. Equally, you should allow at least three minutes of cooling before finally turning the master switch OFF.

The searchlight produces a very intense white light. At a range of about 400 feet its intensity in the 'spot' mode is about the equivalent of bright moonlight. Beam width on the ground will obviously vary depending on slant range, and on whether you have the light in 'spot' or 'flood' mode.

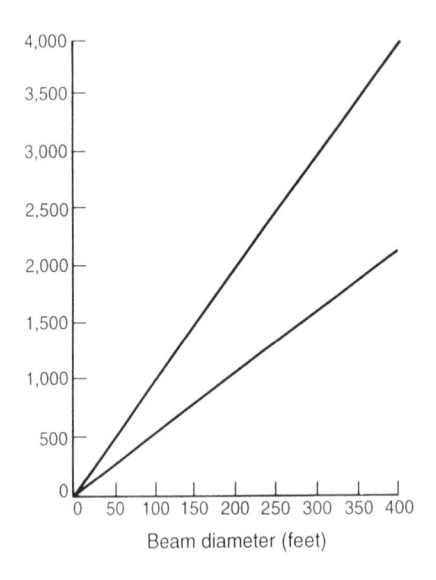

Beam diameter (feet)

Although it is unlikely that you would want to look directly into the beam of the searchlight, you must be aware of the dangers of doing so. The luminance of the searchlight face, when measured at the centre of the beam, has a brilliance approaching that of the sun. If this light were allowed to focus on the retina of your eyes, depending on the distance, retinal burning could result. (Think of the sun, a magnifying glass and a piece of paper.) Such a burn would leave you with a permanent blind spot in your field of vision. **No warning pain would be felt, as there are no pain-sensitive nerves in the retina.** To avoid this danger, never look towards the searchlight face at distances of less than one kilometre.

Forced Landings and Ditching

During your flying training you were taught the rudiments of forced landings. To avoid unnecessary damage to the helicopter, the simulations were probably carried out within reach of easy landing sites. This itself can create a problem when you are faced with a real emergency, as it tempts you to stretch your glide in an attempt to reach an ideal site, whereas the best course may well be to go for a poor site within easy reach and accept the risk of damaging the helicopter.

When a moving object is brought to rest, the violence of the stopping force, expressed in G, depends on speed and stopping distance. Speed in itself is not the killer; the danger lies in how it is dissipated. Many people believe that a very large stopping distance is required to dissipate the speed. Theoretically, it would take only twenty feet to decelerate a helicopter from 100 kts to zero without imposing intolerable levels on the human body. The whole skill lies in spreading the deceleration evenly over the entire stopping space.

The problem in most emergency landings is that the deceleration is not uniform. Whenever a helicopter strikes an obstacle or digs in, peak deceleration occurs, and it is during these peak periods that injury exposure is at its worst. Anything which will even out the deceleration is therefore of the greatest importance.

The human body is fairly resilient and will, when suitably restrained, withstand some high 'G' loadings. The difference in body tolerance between 'G' loads resulting from manoeuvres and the loads imposed in a crash-type deceleration is often not understood.

'G' loads in flight are of sufficiently long duration to affect the blood circulation, and unconsciousness may occur from 4 to 6 'G'. Impact loads are measured in fractions of a second and the body can withstand these to a surprising degree – up to 40 'G' during deceleration perpendicular to the spine and up to 25 'G' parallel to the spine. It cannot handle very well the 'G' forces exerted simultaneously in two different planes. **The correct use of your seat harness is all-important, and cannot be stressed too strongly.**

Some peak 'G' levels under typical accident situations are worth examining:
   a) With a sink rate of 1,500 feet per minute, zero ground speed and touching down on soft ground providing cushioning to a depth of one foot, a force of between 8 and 13 'G' would be experienced.

b) With the same sink rate on to hard ground and with forward ground speed, a peak horizontal deceleration of 15 to 25 'G' would coincide with the peak vertical deceleration due to the increased frictional force while the vertical speed is dissipated. This situation would be marginal.

c) A similar touchdown with forward velocity on to soft ground would almost certainly result in very serious injuries.

Therefore, the less suitable the ground, the more important it is to reduce your forward velocity at touchdown. At the same time, it would be unwise to aim for a zero-speed touchdown if the terrain is suitable for a run-on landing.

Injuries resulting from violent decelerations can be divided into two categories:

Contact Injuries: these result from contact with the environmental structure. This occurs when an inadequate restraint system is used, when loose articles are allowed in the cabin, or when external objects break through into the cockpit.

Deceleration injuries: this term is used to indicate body damage resulting solely from loads applied direct to the body through the occupant's seat and restraint system. Deceleration injuries affect the body internally.

Basically, there are two categories of helicopter emergency landings:

a) Forced Landing: when further level flight is impossible, but not because of catastrophic control problems.

b) Precautionary Landing: when further flight is possible but inadvisable under present conditions, e.g. deteriorating weather, uncertain position, shortage of fuel, etc.

It cannot be too strongly emphasised that the helicopter pilot who understands the problems involved, and the techniques available, is unlikely to expose himself or his passengers to fatal injury during an emergency landing. If serious personal injuries do occur in emergency landings, they generally result from a lack of understanding of the basic mechanics involved, compounded by one or more of the following errors:

a) A reluctance to accept the emergency situation. The pilot who will not accept the fact that his helicopter will be on the ground in a very short time, regardless of what he thinks or hopes, is already handicapping himself. Attempts to delay the inevitable by trying to maintain altitude at the expense of loss of speed and/or rotor revolutions per minute (RRPM) will reduce helicopter controllability.

b) The desire to save the helicopter, even when it implies a

course of action that leaves no margin for error. If all goes well the helicopter may sustain little or no damage. However, if the pilot loses his gamble, the helicopter as well as its occupants may be lost. Over-stretched glides and failure to allow for obstacles in the approach path are typical of the mistakes made under these conditions.
    c) Undue concern about getting hurt in a landing on rough terrain. This can have an adverse effect on a pilot's judgement and technique.

Except for the few critical seconds after transitioning into the climb, the pilot has little excuse for denying himself the choice of an emergency landing site. This is not to suggest that one should fly around preoccupied with the problems of possible engine failure, but one should learn to develop some protective instincts and sound habits.

Route selection: Imagination in planning can go a long way to improving survival prospects. The difference between flying a direct route that leaves little choice in an emergency and one that passes over less-hostile terrain is often only a matter of a few minutes flying or a few more gallons of fuel.

Altitude and Airspeed: More altitude means more choice. Airspeed can also be converted into altitude, which again provides more choice. To fly low and slow over neck-breaking terrain without good reason is wrong.

Trees: Accident experience proves conclusively that in some emergency situations trees can be a helicopter pilot's best friend. In conjunction with the main rotor blades, trees have an energy absorbing capability. In practical terms this means that, under certain circumstances (low RRPM), a tree landing could be even less hazardous than one on flat, open terrain.

Water: Many pilots are reluctant to ditch their helicopter in an emergency. This may be due to the prospect of the helicopter being a total loss, or to a fear of becoming trapped. As far as impact is concerned, ditching presents less of a problem than a landing on very rough terrain or in high trees. Ditching is covered in more detail later on in this chapter.

Emergency landing site selection from altitude is initially based on general appearance and is therefore not always final. As the terrain features become more apparent, the pilot should not be afraid to change to another site that is obviously better. As a general rule you should not change your mind more than once; a well-planned forced landing on to poor ground can be less hazardous than a wild approach to a better site.

Many emergency landings fail because the pilot spends too much time attempting to rectify the problem, instead of giving more time to the planning and execution of the approach. Emergency landing procedure and the control of the helicopter must always take priority over any engine restart drills. Towards the end of the approach the pilot is in the best position to judge the helicopter's remaining manoeuvring capability with respect to the terrain choice, and must make the final decision on the exact touchdown area and the manner of touchdown. Of all the errors that can be made up to this point, one is critical – the loss of RRPM. This can result in the loss of control over the method of touchdown.

The techniques of touchdown vary enormously between open terrain and trees.

Open terrain The helicopter pilot must decide the following:
- a) Does the surface allow a run-on landing?
- b) If a run-on landing is to be made, is there sufficient helicopter control to ensure a touchdown without drifting or rolling?
- c) If the surface conditions are poor, do density altitude, wind and all-up weight permit a zero-speed landing at a reasonable sink rate, or will it have to be a compromise in the form of a minimum run-on?

Tree landings When a tree landing is unavoidable, the following considerations apply:
- a) The height of a tree is less critical than the height above the ground at which it begins to branch. Tall trees with thin tops allow too much free-fall height after the helicopter passes through the branches.
- b) When dealing with young, short trees, the most densely and evenly wooded area should be chosen. This is the ideal situation, as the bottom of the helicopter, as well as the main rotor, provides a cushioning effect.
- c) If at all possible, main rotor contact with heavy trunks high above the ground should be avoided, as it may result in loss of the main rotor or a transmission failure.
- d) A landing in a sparsely wooded area may require more finesse than a landing in a dense forest canopy, as the few individual trees act as obstacles rather than energy absorbers.
- e) Brush-type vegetation of less than helicopter height should be dealt with as if it were not there.
- f) Clearings in woods should be treated with caution, as they

may contain tree stumps and other obstacles that may penetrate the bottom of the helicopter.
  g) Dead trees are dangerous; they offer little energy absorption and there is the risk of cabin penetration.

A tree landing should be executed with zero groundspeed and in a tail-low attitude. If, for any reason, the pilot is unable to reduce the forward velocity to safe limits and tree contact is unavoidable, the helicopter should be flared to an extremely nose-high attitude against the densest growth, and as close to the ground as possible. Under these circumstances he is using the trees to absorb energy in a horizontal plane, and the bottom of the helicopter becomes the main contact point as well as a protective shield.

The correct techniques for ditching are still controversial. What is certain, however, is the need to reduce impact and the fact that the helicopter will float for only a very short time. Before it completely disappears it will almost certainly roll to one side or the other.

In addition to information contained in the relevant Flight Manual, five major aspects should be considered. These are: reading the sea; the approach; the reduction of impact; stopping the rotors; and getting out of the helicopter.

Reading the Sea: The two essentials that must be assessed are the wind and the wave state. These should be assessed when crossing from land to water, and reassessed at least every half-hour thereafter. As the wind is primarily responsible for waves, whitecaps and foam, these signs can be used to determine wind speed. A rough rule of thumb is that when the sea is calm or with only small waves, the wind speed is 0 to 20 kts. With many white caps it is 20 to 30 kts, when streaks of foam appear it is 30 to 40 kts, and when the wave crests give off spray it is 40 to 50 kts.

Swells are the principal danger when ditching. Basically there are two kinds of swell, major and secondary. In-between the major swells are troughs, where secondary swells are found. Major swells are larger than secondary swells. If you have trouble in distinguishing them, major swells will be clearly visible from above 2,000 feet. These are the ones which will most affect your ditching, and it is important that you know which way they are running. The smaller, secondary swells will usually run at an angle to the major system.

The Approach: The following should be considered when selecting a ditching area:
  a) If you are flying near a coastline or an island and a forced landing is inadvisable, ditch in the lee of the land.
  b) Ditch in slightly ruffled water in preference to a calm,

mirror-like surface. Flat, still water makes an accurate assessment of height extremely difficult.
  c) If sea, rather than wind, is the prime consideration, come in to ditch parallel to the swell.
  d) If there is a ship close by, try to ditch beside it. Aim to touch down just behind the bow wave to allow the maximum time to clear the helicopter before the wake appears.

Reduction of Impact: The need to reduce impact is as essential as for a forced landing on land. A zero-speed touchdown with a tail-down entry is the ideal. If the moment of impact can be controlled, aim to enter the rear slope of a wave just below the crest. If ditching parallel to the swells, enter near the crest.

Stopping the Rotors: The main rotors represent the major post-crash hazard. Entering the water in a tail-down attitude means that the reduction of RRPM begins at the earliest possible moment. As the helicopter enters the water, continue raising the collective lever to slow down the main rotor blades. It is possible that as you get to the end of the collective travel, the helicopter will roll over. This could be a natural result of the weight and buoyancy distribution, or might be due to wave action. Current thinking is that, as soon as the helicopter enters the water, the pilot should initiate a roll towards the advancing blade so that the shock will cause the retreating blade to be thrown in a direction to the rear of the cabin and away from the occupants.

Getting Out: There are a number of conflicting factors concerning the doors of the helicopter in preparation for ditching:
  a) With the doors closed, flotation time is slightly longer but inversion may be quicker.
  b) Closed doors may be difficult to jettison if distortion has taken place.
  c) Jettisoning doors before ditching may involve rotor damage and consequent loss of control.

In the author's opinion, if doors are fitted, they should be opened before ditching and the handles turned to the 'shut' position while they are open. Thereafter the door can be safely pulled to, and more easily opened when necessary. If the doors are submerged, even partially, water pressure may prevent them being opened or jettisoned. In this situation, opening the window will help to equalise the pressure as quickly as possible.

If the doors are already off at the time of entry, take a deep breath. There will be a lot of water around immediately. In the event, which way you exit will probably depend on which way the helicopter rolls. It will almost certainly roll before the rotors stop.

More fatalities have been sustained by leaving too early and being struck by the main rotor than by leaving too late. It has been argued that you should wait until the water appears an even green and has lost all trace of being white and foamy.

The impact shock when the rotors strike the water can be very severe, and disorientation will be considerable when the helicopter rolls. Strength of mind is therefore required to keep your safety harness secured until the helicopter settles. Unfastening of harness should be left as late as possible.

When ditching under power the normal procedure is:
 a) Establish a normal hover and evacuate all passengers, and
 b) Hover a safe distance to one side and downwind of the evacuees and ditch the helicopter.

The time to prepare for ditching is not in the air after it becomes necessary, but on the ground before take-off.

Winter Operations

Many helicopter students aim to complete their flying training during the summer months to take advantage of the longer daylight hours and the more settled weather. Although this has many plus points, it does not prepare them for operating in the winter months.

If a helicopter is parked outside in the winter, the residual heat in the various parts of the airframe and engine will be dissipated to the atmosphere. The rate of heat dissipation, and hence the reduction in temperature, will depend upon the amount of heat to be dissipated and the rate at which it is being extracted. It follows, therefore, that a large mass such as a main rotor gearbox will cool at a much slower rate than a tail-rotor gearbox, which is a smaller mass. The rate of cooling will depend largely on the wind-chill factor, so heat will be extracted faster from those parts which are directly exposed.

The minimum temperature to which a helicopter may be reduced without sustaining damage – mainly to seals in the oil, hydraulic and fuel systems – is usually referred to in the helicopter's documentation as the minimum **cold soak** temperature.

If a helicopter has been parked outside in the cold, then, in addition to the normal pre-flight checks the pilot should also:

Ensure that all snow, ice and frost is removed from the helicopter, including the main and tail rotors.

Inspect the main rotorhead to ensure that no particles of ice or hard snow could cause jamming of the controls.

Inspect all fuel tank vents for icing.

Check that all air intakes are free of snow and ice.

Defrost the windscreen and windows.

Most helicopters have other overriding limits above the 'cold soak' temperature for starting the engine. If the helicopter has been cold soaked down to or near to its minimum temperature, then pre-heating should be considered as a way of bringing the engine and transmission oil temperatures up to the minimum for starting. Engine starting during very cold weather is always easier if the engine and transmission are pre-heated. Always try to use an external start if possible, to reduce the drain on the battery. Batteries lose a large percentage of their capacity at low temperatures.

Special precautions are needed when you are ground-running on ice- or snow-covered surfaces, to prevent the helicopter from sliding around. Gentle control movements are essential. Harsh usage of the throttle can be particularly dangerous. Care must also be taken regarding the position of the cyclic stick, as small rotor deflections can cause the helicopter to slide.

When lifting off from snow, the rotor downwash can create a large snow cloud which can lead to a possible loss of reference, or **white-out**. Because of this, the recommended technique is to use a towering take-off, as this minimises the critical period in the snow cloud.

The main problem of flying over snow covered terrain is that your sense of depth perception is greatly reduced. The main effects are that:

It reduces your ability to judge height.

It reduces the impression of speed, which is normally obtained when you are flying near to the ground.

It increases the collision-with-the-ground hazard by obscuring any higher ground on track.

With reduced visibility, the combination can result in the total loss of horizon (white-out), requiring you to revert to instrument flying.

White-out is a disorientation problem. It can occur when a fresh snowfall or blowing snow has whitened the terrain to an even tone. With clear skies there is usually sufficient shadow and contrast to provide adequate reference. In heavy overcast conditions the problem is increased, especially if precipitation or low cloud limits the horizon reference.

The most difficult condition occurs when the sky is obscured with an even, light overcast, and when blowing snow is present. This produces glare which is then reflected in all directions and obscures all shadow contrast, thus making it almost impossible to detect relief even when the helicopter is very close to the ground.

Close attention should be paid in flight to your transmission and engine oil temperatures, to ensure that they do not fall below permissible limits, especially during a long descent. High airspeed and low power produce the lowest engine oil temperatures.

In spite of heating and demisting systems, windscreen and windows are prone to internal frosting, particularly during descents. Although it can be uncomfortable, opening a window is often the best solution to ensure safe visibility.

Icing is the most serious effect of low-temperature operations. If all water droplets froze immediately the temperature fell below 0°C, ice formation could easily be prevented simply by avoiding the freezing level. Unfortunately, water droplets can remain liquid well below 0°C. Such droplets are then said to be 'supercooled' and are unstable. If they collide with any solid, freezing occurs. The heaviest accretions take place at temperatures between -1°C and

−15°C. After this the air begins to dry out. However, ice can form at ambient temperatures well above freezing point owing to a local temperature drop caused by disturbances of airflow.

Although rotor icing can occur without airframe icing, the presence of ice on visible external parts of the airframe is an almost certain indication that icing is occurring on the rotors.

Always try to select a large open site for the landing. The main problems that might be encountered on the approach to land are estimating the wind, judging height and the effects of recirculation.

Recirculation is the major hazard. Opinions differ regarding the best technique to minimise it. Running landings in an attempt to retain a clear field of view should be avoided, as relatively high touchdown speeds are required to keep the recirculating snow behind the helicopter. They also make it difficult to detect any slope or snow-hidden objects.

The best advice is to keep the helicopter moving forward and down to complete a zero- or low-speed landing. Always be prepared for the effects of white-out as you get close to the ground, and be ready to initiate an overshoot if necessary.

After landing and shutdown, always try to fit the covers and blanks straight away to conserve heat and reduce engine and transmission cooling and, if possible, fill the fuel tanks to prevent internal condensation.

Visual Searches

There will be times when a pilot will need to search for an object, or will be requested to assist in locating something on behalf of someone else. One of the main factors that will affect the search plan is the **detection distance (D)**. This is the maximum distance at which the object may be located from the air under any given set of conditions. Visual detection will be affected by meteorological visibility, the size of the object, the colour of the object in relation to the background, the nature of the terrain and the height of the search helicopter.

It is almost impossible to predict the visual detection distance over land of an object, as it will vary according to the prevailing conditions. As an example, however, a dinghy at sea in reasonable visibility should have a visual detection distance of about ½ nm from a height of 800 feet.

Three main search patterns that should be considered: the parallel track search, the creeping line ahead search, and the square

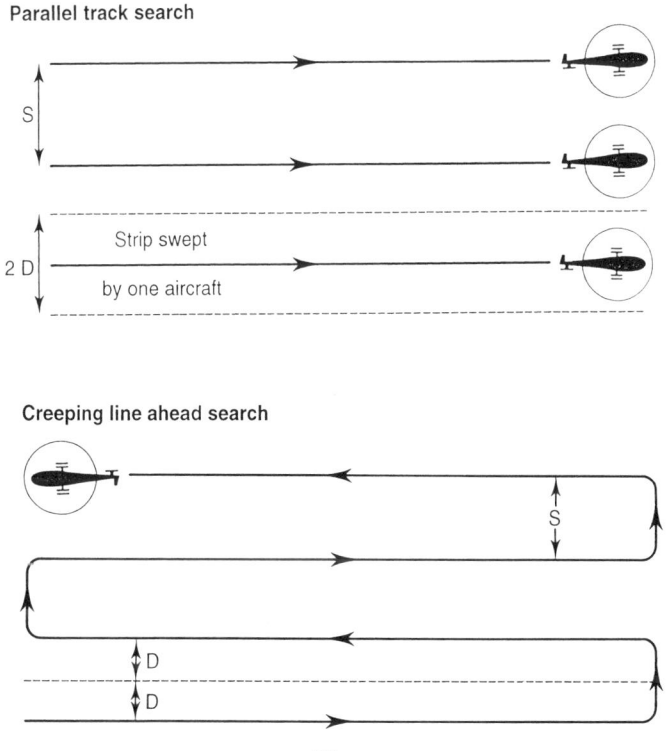

Parallel track search

S

2 D
Strip swept
by one aircraft

Creeping line ahead search

S

D
D

Square search

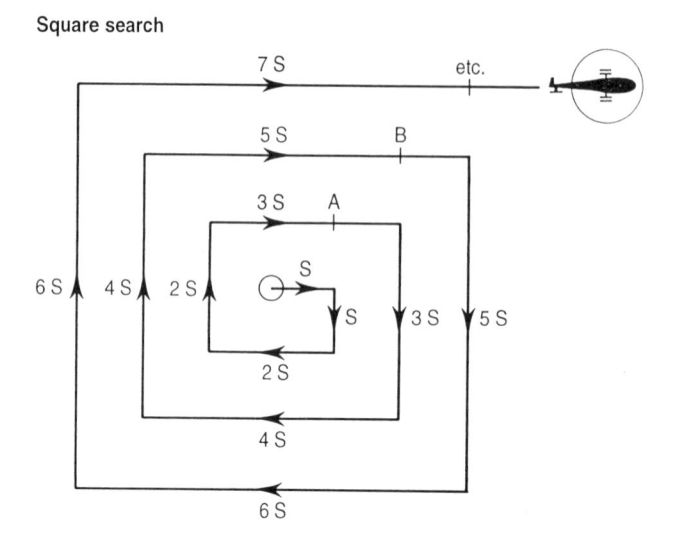

search. In all of these patterns the essential factor is the detection distance (D), as this will normally dictate your **track spacing (S)**. This will normally be double the detection distance.

The parallel track search is usually carried out with two or more helicopters flying parallel tracks.

The creeping line ahead search pattern consists of parallel tracks spaced at a distance of 2D apart and joined by short tracks.

The square search pattern covers an area with a series of repeated expanded squares whose sides are spaced 2D apart. The length of the side of the square is increased by the distance of the track spacing after every two sides have been flown. At point A, one square has been completed, at point B two squares, and so on. To make your navigation easier, try to arrange your tracks to line up, down and across the wind.

Winching

All winching is a joint operation between the pilot and the winch operator. It is essential, therefore, that there is an unambiguous and standard procedure which will allow winching to be carried out safely and speedily.

Before undertaking any form of winching, both the pilot and winch operator must have completed a proper course of instruction with a Qualified Helicopter Instructor.

In addition to the normal All-Up Weight and CG calculations, the pilot must also ensure that the Lateral CG will be within limits with a load on the hoist hook.

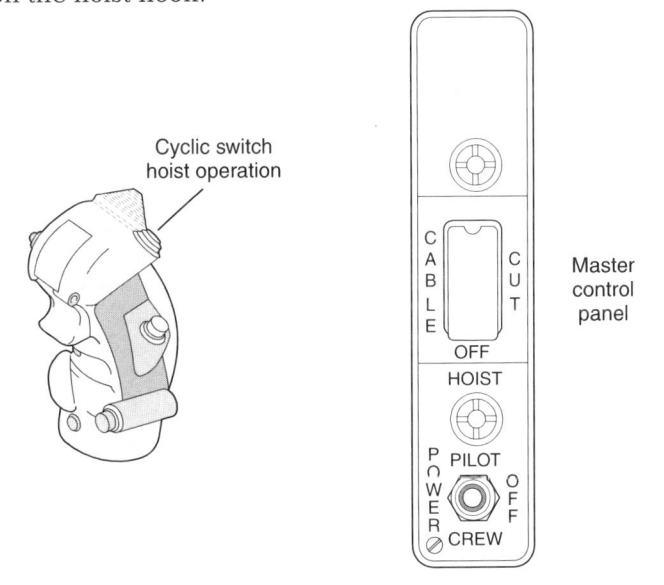

It is essential in all types of lifting that if the immediate safety of the helicopter is endangered by the winch cable or load being caught by an obstruction, that the pilot be able to cut the wire by means of a cable cutter.

It is the pilot's responsibility to ensure that the cable cutter guard functions correctly and that all personnel involved are fully briefed on the cable cutter control.

Before flight, the operation of the winch should be checked using both the pilot's and the winch operator's controls. The hook should also be checked for serviceability and to ensure that it is free to rotate about the swivel.

Rubber bumper

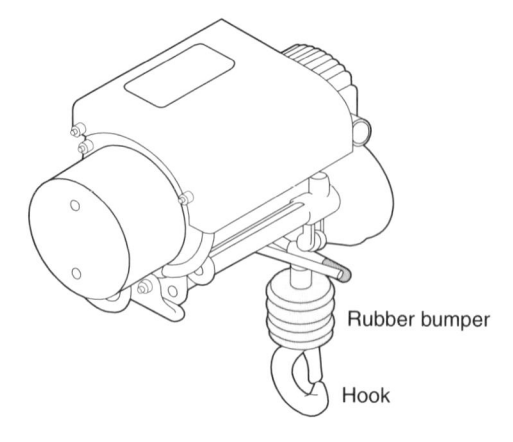

Hook

All other lifting and safety equipment to be used must also be thorougly checked out.

The lifting and lowering of loads will normally be carried out from a hover. An exception to this is when time-saving is operationally vital, in which case a single descending live load may be partially lowered during the approach to the site.

One of the critical stages in winching is immediately after the load has been hoisted inboard. The period during which the load is neither secured to the hoist nor internally restrained should be reduced to a minimum. A protective winch operator's arm across the doorway will do much to ensure live load safety at this stage.

The winch operator should only winch out sufficient cable for the task. Whilst in the hover he will be winching in and out continuously to correct minor inaccuracies in the position of the helicopter.

It can be just as bad to have excess cable out as it is to have insufficient. Whilst personnel are being attached to the lifting equipment the cable should be very slightly slack. Prior to lifting off by the helicopter the cable should be taut.

The winch operator should work the winch with his right hand and guide the winch cable with his left. Any oscillations can be damped out by exerting pressure on the cable in the opposite direction.

A **Single Live Lift** is used to lower/raise trained or fully briefed personnel. A strop, which is attached to the winch hook, is placed over the head, under the armpits and secured by pulling down the sliding toggle to the chest. The winch operator must check for correct fitment.

The person being winched down will sit on the edge of the cabin floor, legs over the sill. At the winch operator's command he will swing himself under the winch holding the webbing of the strop above the toggle. When steady, the winch operator will gently extend the cable, at the same time steadying it with a gloved hand to prevent undue oscillations.

When getting out of the strop, the person being lowered must avoid being struck by the heavy weight above the winch hook.

For winching up, the strop is put on in a similar manner. When it is correctly fitted, the 'SECURE' signal is given to the winch operator, who will then commence to winch up until the load is level with the cabin floor.

He will then turn the person to face away from the cabin, place his left arm around his waist and pull him into the cabin in the sitting position – winching out slightly if necessary.

A **Double Live Lift** is used to raise untrained personnel. The **rescue strop** is first placed on the hook followed by the **winchman's strop**.

The winch operator, after checking security, lowers the winchman down to the surface.

The winchman then secures the person to be lifted into the rescue strop and gives the 'SECURE' signal.

The winch operator then instructs the pilot, 'UP GENTLY', and when clear of the surface commences to winch up the two people on the hook.

The winchman faces the other person and secures him with his legs in a 'scissors' grip. He uses his hands to guide himself and the other person through the skid gear of the helicopter. On reaching the cabin door the winchman turns the person so that they are facing away from the cabin. he then grasps the door frame with his right hand and with his feet on the door sill, eases the person into the cabin.

The winch operator can assist at this stage by pulling in around the person's waist.

The **Standard Winching Circuit** as shown is normally only practised under training conditions. However, the procedures, checks and calls are invariably used on operational flights, even if the actual position where they are used has to be modified.

All turns are normally made in the direction which allows the pilot and crew members the best view of the target. During the last part of the run in to the hover the pilot will lose sight of the target and from then on has to rely on the verbal picture given to him by the winch operator.

The winch operator can, by using standard voice procedure, direct the pilot overhead the target. The pilot, by making the corrections stated by the winch operator, can maintain the helicopter overhead the target until the winching operation is completed.

It is essential that all crew members act as a team and, by using standard procedures, avoid confusion.

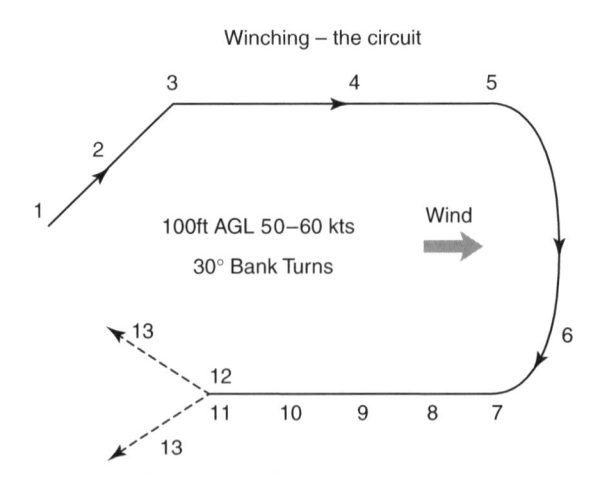

Winching – the circuit

100ft AGL 50–60 kts

30° Bank Turns

Position	Action
1. Target sighting	The target is identified to all crew members by clock reference and distance in metres.
2. Approaching target	Pilot performs power checks to ensure sufficient margin for winching.
3. Downwind	Downwind checks. Normal circuit 100 feet AGL, 50–60 kts.
4. Downwind	Checks complete. Winch operator states what items are attached to the hook and type of lift to be undertaken.
5. Turning on	Pilot commences a slow descent in the turn. Winch operator gives heading of target.
6. Turning on	Pilot reduces height and speed (20–25 feet above obstacles, 25–30 kts ground speed).
7. Running up	Pilot heads into wind towards target. Winch operator gives range in metres, (normally starts from 200).
8. Target sighted	Pilot informs winch operator 'target in sight'. Under direction of winch operator reduces height. Winch operator continues to direct pilot.
9. Winching out	At about 40 metres the winch operator winches out, if time is critical, and gives range and line direction to the pilot.
10. Approach to hover	Winch operator winches out to make contact with surface to earth the static electricity build up.
11. Hover	The pilot maintains his position by making the corrections stated by the winch operator. On the 'Up gently' the pilot raises the helicopter so as to lift the load clear of the surface.
12. Hover	The winch operator winches in, aiming to keep the load not more than 15–20 feet AGL by directing the pilot to descend gently.
13. Winching complete	Winch operator informs the pilot when the winching is complete. The pilot climbs away or into another circuit as required.

The winch operator's directions to the pilot must be clear and concise. All distances are given in metres, being the individual operator's estimate. Line and height corrections are given especially in the final stages of the approach. Any corrections ordered must be cancelled by 'Dead Ahead', 'Hold Your Height' or 'Steady' to avoid any confusion on the pilot's part.

Whilst the load is being raised or lowered, the winch operator must give the pilot a word picture of what is happening outside the helicopter.

The **Standard Voice Procedures for Winching**:

Serial	Pilot	Winch Operator	Meaning Action
1	'Target sighted ... o'clock ... metres'	'Contact'	Target indicated by clock reference from helicopter. If winch operator identifies target first, the sequence is reversed.
2	'Power sufficient'	'Roger'	Power check complete.
3	'Downwind'	'Roger'	
4	'Fuel at ... lb. Cable cutter guarded, selected and master ON'	'Checks complete. Attached to the hook is ...'	Pilot's D/W checks acknowledged by winch operator, who informs him what type of lift is to be done.
5	'Turning on'	'Turning on. Target at ... o'clock'	Commencing turn to run in. Winch operator calls position from 3 o'clock, 2 o'clock, 1 o'clock and dead ahead.
6	'Running up'	'Running up'	Final approach.
7	'Target sighted'	'Roger'	This can occur earlier in the circuit if necessary.
8		'Forward 100; descend'	Pilot has approx 100 metres to run. Should continue descent.

9	'Forward 80. Hold your height'	Pilot has approx 80 metres to run. Height is correct.
10	'Forward 60'	Pilot has approx 60 metres to run.
11	'Forward 40. Winching out' (if time is vital)	Pilot has approx 40 metres to run. Winch being lowered.
12	'Up ... (feet)' 'Down ... (feet)' 'Hold your height'	Height corrections given in units of 5 at any time. Always cancelled by 'Hold your height'.
13	'Forward 30, 20, 15, 10, 8, 6, 5, 4, 3, 2, 1'	Continue to give range to pilot.
14	'Left ... (metres)' 'Right ... (metres)' 'Dead ahead'	Line corrections given in units of 1 during latter stages. Always cancelled by 'Dead ahead'
15	'Steady'	Over the target. It will always follow a successful correction by the pilot.
16	'Back 1' 'Forward 2' 'Right 1' 'Left 3'	Minor corrections given by the winch operator to keep the helicopter over the target.
17		The winch operator gives the pilot a continuous word picture of the progress of the winching.
18	'Up gently'	Raise the helicopter to lift the load clear of the surface.

19		'Clear of the ground. Winching in'	Helicopter to hold its height. Load being winched up.
20		'Clear to descend slowly'	Descend over the spot whilst load is being winched in.
21		'Winching in. 10 to come'	Winching in with 10 feet to go.
22		'Top of the arm. Bringing inboard'	Load about to come into the cabin.
23		'Inboard. Winching complete'	Pilot can move into forward flight.
24	'I have control of the winch'	'You have control of the winch'	Pilot wishes to work winch under directions of winch operator.
25		'Chop, Chop, Chop'	Cut the cable.
26		'Up, Up, Up'	Climb. Helicopter is dangerously low.

Some additional **Hand Signals for Winching Operations**:

Signal	Meaning
1. Extend one arm with the thumb up and look at the winch operator.	Secure and ready for winching in.
2. A slow patting motion with the palm of the hand down (arm extended).	Winch out more cable.
3. An up and down motion of the hand with the palm up.	Winch in some cable.
4. The hand stationary with the palm towards the winch operator.	Stop winching.

5. Draw the edge of the hand across the throat with a cutting motion — Emergency advisory signal that the cable should be cut.

Some **General Precautions** to be followed when undertaking a winching task:

1. A minimum lift of 15 to 20 feet is recommended, as hovering below this height does not allow sufficient time to fire the cable cutter in the event of an emergency.

2. Be aware of any restrictions on the number of lifts that can be carried out with any one cable. The winch operator should always be looking for any signs of deterioration of the cable – fraying, kinking or unravelling.

3. Where a danger of static electricity exists, the cable should be earthed by allowing it to touch the ground immediately prior to attaching a live load. In the case of a double lift, an extension conductor will be necessary. With a dead load normal probe earthing should be adopted similar to underslung load operations.

4. The heavy weight on the winch hook can be highly lethal when swinging free and all concerned must be warned of this danger.

5. All passengers and crew members must be adequately secured at all times.

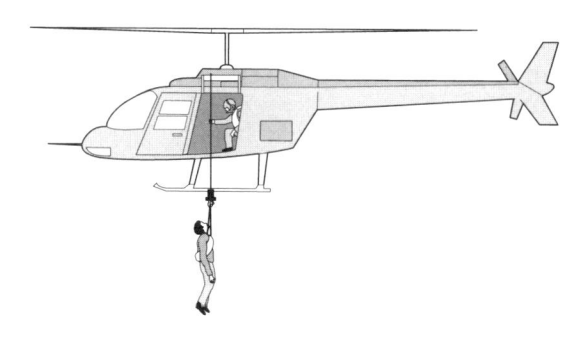

Index

180° turns 33, 34, 36

AAI (angle of approach indicator) 56–58
ASI (airspeed indicator) 6
airframe 5
airspeed indicator (ASI) 6
altitude, density 5, 16
angle of approach indicator (AAI) 56–58
apprehension 4
approach speed 24
approaches 23–24
  to crests and peaks 30–32
  to slope landing sites 28
  to valley landing sites 34–35
area of nil or zero wind 13
arms, measuring 45–46
attitude appreciation, loss of 3

balance 43–46
  calculation 46–48
blade stall 6, 17

C of G see Centre of Gravity
cargo hooks 50
Centre of Gravity (C of G) 43–44
  calculation 46, 48
  forward and aft limits 44–45
circuit of landing site 22
cols, flights through 36
crest line, crossing 29
crests 29–32
  approaches to 30–32
  flights over 29–30
  take-offs from 32

datum, reference 43, 45–46
decision point 24
demarcation line 7, 8, 10, 12, 20

density altitude 5, 16
detection distance, visual 73, 74
ditchings 65, 67–69
  approach 67–68
  getting out 68–69
  reading the sea 67
  reduction of impact 68
  stopping the rotors 68
  under power 69
downdraughts 8, 10, 12, 13, 14, 17–18, 20

electrically grounding 50–51, 83
emergency landings see forced landings
engine failure 17
engine power 5

flares 58–60
flight controls, response of 6
flight preparation 16
flights
  along slopes 26–28
  in and along valleys 33–35
  over crests 29–30
  through cols 36
forced landings 63–69 see also ditchings
  errors causing injuries 64–65
  injuries resulting from 64
  landing site selection 65
  open terrain 66
  tree landings 65, 66–67
fuel weight 42

'G' loads 63–64
'Gs' (load factors) 40
gust spread 9

helicopter balance 43–46

calculation 46–48
helicopter considerations 5–6
helicopter performance charts, study of 16
helicopter weight 40–42
  calculation 46–48
hooks, cargo 50
horizon, disappearance of normal 3

laminar flow 9
landing sites 18, 19–22
  determining wind direction and behaviour at 19–21
  emergency 65
  reconnaissance of 21–22
  on slopes 27
  in valleys 34
landing technique, sight 23–24, 35
landings 24
  forced *see* forced landings
Lateral C of G reference datum 43–44, 75
load factors ('Gs') 40
load lifting signals 51–53
load oscillations 53–55
loading calculation, sample 46–47
loads, underslung 49–55
  landing with 55
  lifting 53
  stacking 49

maps, study of 16
medical factors 3–4
meteorological conditions, study of 16
moments 45, 46
mountain flying common faults 38
mountain winds 7–15
mountains, en route to 17–18

night landing system 56
night operations 56–62

Nightsun searchlight *see* searchlight, Nightsun
nil wind, area of 13

oscillations, load 53–55
oxygen 4

passenger weights 42
peaks, approaches to 30–32
  see also crests
pinnacles 29–32
power margin 19

reconnaissance of landing sites 21–22
  on slopes 27–28
  in valleys 34
reference datum 43, 45–46
ridges, multiple 12
rolls 9, 10, 12
rotor, tail 5
rotor cloud 15
rotor streaming turbulence 14–15
rotors 5
route selection 65

searches, visual 73–74
searchlight, Nightsun 60–62
  danger of looking into 62
  operation 61–62
shadow, effect of 37
sharp contours 12
signals, load lifting 51–53
signals, winching hand 82–83
slopes 10–11
  flying along 26–28
  landing sites on 27–28
snow *see* winter operations
stable layer 14–15
standing waves 13–14
static electricity 50–51, 83
sun, effect of 37
swivels 49–50

tail rotor 5

85

take-offs 25
 from crests 32
 from valleys 34–35
temperature, minimum cold soak 70
terms, commonly used 41
transition point 7
trees, forced landings in 65, 66–67
turbulence 8, 9, 11, 13, 14, 40
turbulence, rotor streaming 14–15
turbulence penetration airspeed 17

updraughts 10, 12, 14, 16, 20

valleys, flights in and along 33–35
valleys, landing sites in 34–35
venturi effect 10
vertigo 3
visual searches 73–74

weight, basic empty 41–42
weight, helicopter 40–42
 calculation 46–48
weight checks 42
white-out 71, 72
winching 75–83

Double Live Lift 77–78
general precautions 83
hand signals 82–83
pre-flight checks 75–76
Single Live Lift 76–77
Standard Voice Procedures 80–82
Standard Winching Circuit 78–79
winch operator 76, 77, 80
wind assessment 17
wind behaviour 7–9
 windspeed bands 8
wind behaviour and direction at landing site, determining 19–21
 cloverleaf pattern 20–21
 constant airspeed/constant power 20
winds, mountain 7–15
winter operations 70–72
 engine and transmission temperatures 71
 flying in snow 71–72
 ground-running on snow 70–71
 icing 71–72
 pre-flight checks 70

zero wind, area of 13